PIERRE TEILHARD DE CHARDIN'S
PHILOSOPHY OF EVOLUTION

Publication Number 852

AMERICAN LECTURE SERIES®

A Monograph in

The BANNERSTONE DIVISION *of*
AMERICAN LECTURES IN PHILOSOPHY

Edited by

MARVIN FARBER
State University of New York at Buffalo
Buffalo, New York

Pierre Teilhard De Chardin's
Philosophy of Evolution

By

H. JAMES BIRX Ph.D.

Department of Anthropology
Canisius College
Buffalo, New York

CHARLES C THOMAS · PUBLISHER
Springfield · Illinois · U.S.A.

Published and Distributed Throughout the World by

CHARLES C THOMAS • PUBLISHER

BANNERSTONE HOUSE

301-327 East Lawrence Avenue, Springfield, Illinois, U.S.A.

© *1972, by* CHARLES C THOMAS • PUBLISHER

ISBN 0-398-02466-9

Library of Congress Catalog Card Number: 72-190313

With THOMAS BOOKS *careful attention is given to all details of manufacturing and design. It is the Publisher's desire to present books that are satisfactory as to their physical qualities and artistic possibilities and appropriate for their particular use.* THOMAS BOOKS *will be true to those laws of quality that assure a good name and good will.*

Printed in the United States of America

N-10

To Marvin Farber

INSCRIPTION

THE CLIMAX of the opposition to modern education and its foundation, advanced natural philosophy, is reached, of course, in the Church. . . . The most dangerous of the three great enemies of reason and knowledge is not malice, but ignorance, or, perhaps, indolence. The gods themselves still strive in vain against these two latter influences when they have happily vanquished the first.

One of the main supports of that reactionary system is still what we may call "anthropism." I designate by this term "that powerful and world-wide group of erroneous opinions which opposes the human organism to the whole of the rest of nature, and represents it to be the preordained end of the organic creation, an entity essentially distinct from it, a godlike being." Closer examination of this group of ideas shows it to be made up of three different dogmas, which we may distinguish as the *anthropocentric,* the *anthropomorphic,* and the *anthropolatrous.*

ERNST HAECKEL
The Riddle of the Universe
Chapter 1

PREFACE

The PHILOSOPHY of evolution is a very important but often neglected field of rigorous inquiry. Yet the doctrine of organic evolution has had a profound influence on interpretations of the universe in general, and man's place in nature in particular. (The fixity or immutability of species had been held by Plato, Aristotle, Augustine, Aquinas, Kant, and Hegel.) Although evolutionary concepts had been present in Eastern and pre-Socratic thought, Lamarck may be credited with the first significant formulation of the theory.

The past two centuries have seen an amazing amount of empirical evidence amassed to substantiate the doctrine of organic evolution. Evolution has even been extended to include galactic, solar, geological, social, and psychological phenomena as well as biological species. Like Teilhard, some have represented the whole cosmos within an evolutionary model. We may even speak of the evolution of our understanding and interpretations of evolution.

With the gradual acceptance of the doctrine of evolution, scientists, philosophers, and theologians have had to reorient their interpretations of man and nature from the static Greek, medieval, and pre-evolutionary views. To an objective thinker, the scientific evidence supporting the doctrine of organic evolution is conclusive, e.g. biogeography, paleontology, comparative anatomy and vestigial organs, comparative embryology, comparative physiology and biochemistry, comparative psychology and behavior, taxonomy, and population genetics.

The increasing understanding of the mechanisms of the evolution of allele pools, the structure and function of the DNA and RNA molecules, and the laboratory synthesis of amino acids allows population genetics to supplement the selective factors of

Darwinism. In short, the erroneous assumptions of Lamarckism are replaced by neo-Darwinism.

Philosophers and theologians have to acknowledge organic evolution as a firmly established fact, for in the last analysis it is the central concept that holds contemporary biology together. Yet one must distinguish between the *fact* of evolution and the variety of *interpretations* presented.

Philosophy is viewed as critical, synthetic, interpretive thinking which is science-oriented and subject to the canons of logic. The special sciences and philosophy are needed for a proper understanding of evolution; the accumulation of established facts sets limits to speculation without eliminating its significance. Knowledge is always subject to future verification, modification, or falsification. Therefore, there is always a need to critically evaluate our models, concepts, and values. The implications of conceptual frameworks must always be critically reassessed.

We can no longer hold to the fixed nature of man or the world. From a cosmic and evolutionary perspective, man and the earth no longer occupy a privileged position in the universe. Man is now seen as a product of and totally within physical nature. In short, man is a fragment of the material universe.

The author maintains that the universe is monistic, materialistic, relativistic, probabilistic, eternal, and infinitely infinite. Likewise, it is self-sufficient, self-sustaining, and self-creative. The emergence of man with reflective consciousness is a recent planetary event. As such, the natural or physical world is prior to and independent of human experience. Ontologically, human experience and physical objects represent temporal distinctions within a space-time-matter continuum (there are no ontological separations in the universe) . The impact of the special sciences on philosophy can no longer be ignored. And it must be demonstrated that theological considerations are also required for a valid interpretation of man and the world.

The present work was written during 1971, the centennial year of the appearance of Darwin's *The Descent of Man*. It is hoped that it will shed light on clarifying man's true place in the universe.

H. JAMES BIRX

INTRODUCTION

FATHER Pierre Teilhard de Chardin, S.J. (1881-1955) was a very remarkable man. He dedicated his life to scientific research and the love of a personal God. His writings, especially *The Phenomenon of Man,* were an attempt to reconcile within an evolutionary perspective the special sciences, philosophy, and theology, matter and spirit, thought and action, personalism and collectivism, plurality and unity, pantheism and theism, and the facts and implications of evolution with the supernatural elements of Christianity.

As a result of Teilhard's personal but unsuccessful request for the publication of a slightly revised edition of *The Phenomenon of Man,* Pope Pius XII issued an Encyclical Letter, *Humani Generis* (August 12, 1950). The Encyclical Letter gave priority to Divine Revelation (Holy Scripture) and Thomism, warning that evolutionary opinions may be erroneous, i.e. fictitious or conjectural.

The Encyclical Letter held that evolutionism results from a desire to be novel, and therefore the doctrine is merely a question of hypotheses or a "false science." It warned that evolutionism leads to the formless and unstable tenets of a new philosophy and sterile speculation, claiming the major error to be a too free interpretation of the historical books of the Old Testament. In short, the Encyclical Letter held the doctrine of evolution to be not only plainly at variance with Holy Scripture, but to be false by experience as well.

That such a position was a direct attack against Teilhard's new philosophy is obvious:

> Some imprudently and indiscreetly hold that evolution, which has not been fully proved even in the domain of natural sciences, explains the origin of all things, and audaciously support the monistic and pantheistic opinions that the world is in continual evolution . . . for the Catholic faith obliges us to hold that souls are immediately creat-

ed by God. However this must be done in such a way that the reasons
for both opinions, that is, those favorable and those unfavorable to
evolution, be weighed and judged with the necessary seriousness,
moderation and measure, and provided that all are prepared to sub-
mit to the judgment of the Church, to whom Christ has given the
mission of interpreting authentically the Sacred Scriptures and of
defending the dogmas of faith. Some however rashly transgress this
liberty of discussion, when they act as if the origin of the human
body from pre-existing and living matter were already completely
certain and proved by the facts which have been discovered up to
now and by reasoning on those facts, and as if there were nothing in
the sources of divine revelation which demands the greatest moderation and caution in this question.[1]

It was against such a dogmatic position that Teilhard attempted
to establish a better Christianity, i.e. a meta-Christianity within a
cosmic and evolutionary perspective.

It is worth noting that his writings never received the *Nihil
Obstat* and *Imprimatur* which declare that a book or pamphlet is
considered to be free from doctrinal or moral error in the eyes of
the Roman Catholic Church. Likewise, not only was the publication of the papal encyclical *Humani Generis* (1950) implicitly an
attack against the unorthodox thoughts of Teilhard, but a *Moni-
tum* decree (June 30, 1962) issued by the Holy Office on his
works warned bishops and heads of seminaries of the doctrinal
errors inherent in Teilhard's interpretations. It is outrageous that
in the twentieth century a brilliant and gentle mind like Teilhard's would have to suffer silencing by the Roman Catholic
Church because of its curiosity and originality.

The sudden enthusiasm given to Teilhard's posthumously
published works was nothing short of being phenomenal. But a
proper analysis and evaluation of his unique synthesis was not
forthcoming. Scientists referred to it as primarily religious and
mystical, while theologians objected to its unorthodoxy, and

---

[1]Pope Pius XII: *Humani Generis: Concerning Some False Opinions Which
Threaten to Undermine the Foundations of Catholic Doctrine.* Washington, D.C.,
National Catholic Welfare Conference, pp. 4, 16-17. The position of the Encyclical Letter is unwarranted in light of the conclusive scientific evidence supporting the doctrine of evolution.

philosophers, for the most part, ignored it. The truth is that Teilhard has gone far beyond any other philosopher of evolution in trying to reconcile the special sciences, philosophy, and religion.

It is unfortunate that before his death Teilhard's writings were never subject to criticism that would have eliminated the many ambiguities. Now, sixteen years after his death, Teilhard's thought still remains very controversial. Evaluations of its importance vary enormously. Strongly negative evaluations include those made by George Gaylord Simpson, Jacques Maritain, and P. B. Medawar. But at the other extreme are those who, like Theodosius Dobzhansky and Sir Julian Huxley, highly praise Teilhard's attempt at an evolutionary synthesis.

Simpson referred to Teilhard as a "phenomenal man," for as "an accomplished theologian and scientist" he uniquely combined in one well-integrated personality a religious mystic and a natural scientist. In his review of *The Phenomenon of Man,* Simpson wrote:

> Teilhard was *primarily* a Christian mystic and only secondarily, although importantly, a scientist. . . . Teilhard's book is not, however, strictly or even mainly concerned with describing the factual course of evolution. . . . Hence we have a book submitted purely as a scientific treatise and yet devoted to a thesis admittedly undemonstrable scientifically.[2]

And because of Teilhard's religious orientation, Simpson concluded:

> It cannot be argued that this approach from metaphysical or religious premises is *ipso facto* illegitimate. It is, however, proper to insist that its conclusions should not be presented as scientific, and that when they are materially testable they should be submitted to that scientific discipline. . . . This book provides a fascinating glimpse into the mind of a great soul, a kindly man and a subtle mystic. It may prove to be psychologically and historically important if, as is quite possible, it eventuates in a new religious cult of mystical evolutionism. It may do good (but could also conceivably do harm) in forcing theologians to face the fact of evolution more squarely. Despite its own claims it should not be taken either as a scientific

---

[2]George Gaylord Simpson: On the Remarkable Testament of the Jesuit Paleontologist Pierre Teilhard de Chardin. *Sci Amer, 202*:202; 1960.

treatise on evolution or as a derivation of religious conclusions from scientific premises.[3]

His latest evaluation remained unchanged:

> Teilhard's beliefs as to the course and the causes of evolution are not scientifically acceptable, because they are not in truth based on scientific premises and because to the moderate extent that they are subject to scientific tests they fail those tests.[4]

Simpson's comments may mislead readers into believing that there is no scientific merit in Teilhard's works.

Jacques Maritain, the leading Thomist in contemporary philosophy, held that Teilhard had, in fact, given "to Science a dazzling primacy," and as a result had committed an irreparable "sin against the intellect." He referred to Teilhard's work as a "theology-fiction," and wrote:

> The religious experience of Père Teilhard was not transmissible, that's perfectly true, but Teilhardism *is* transmissible, and it transmits itself extremely well, with words, confused ideas, a mystico-philosophical imagery, and a whole emotional commotion of huge illusory hopes, which a good many men of good faith are ready to accept as a genuinely exalting intellectual synthesis and a new theology. . . . For when all is said and done, it was nothing for Marx and Engels to turn Hegel upside down, but to turn Christianity upside down, so that it is no longer rooted in the Trinity and the Redemption but in the evolving Cosmos is quite a different matter. No theologian, mystic, or meditative scholar, no matter how hard he tries, is equal to that—nor even a wonder-worker. . . . One doesn't expect a poem to bring us any kind of rational knowledge whatever, be it scientific, philosophical, or theological. . . . But then there would have been no Teilhardism, or mad hope for the advent of a better Christianity celebrating the glories of the cosmos.[5]

But the strongest rejection of Teilhard's thought came from P. B. Medawar. He held it to be an antiscientific, unintelligible, and impractical philosophy-fiction, containing "a feeble argument, abominably expressed":

---

[3]*Ibid.*, pp. 206, 207.

[4]George Gaylord Simpson: *This View of Life: The World of an Evolutionist.* New York, Harcourt, Brace and World, 1964, p. 232.

[5]Jacques Maritain: Teilhard de Chardin and Teilhardism. *U. S. Catholic, 33*:9, 10; 1967.

Yet the greater part of it . . . is nonsense, tricked out by a variety of tedious metaphysical conceits, and its author can be excused of dishonesty only on the grounds that before deceiving others he has taken great pains to deceive himself. *The Phenomenon of Man* cannot be read without a feeling of suffocation, a grasping and flailing around for sense. . . . I have read and studied *The Phenomenon of Man* with real distress, even with despair. Instead of wringing our hands over the Human Predicament, we should attend to those parts of it which are wholly remediable, above all to the gullibility which makes it possible for people to be taken in by such a bag of tricks as this. If it were an innocent, passive gullibility it would be excusable; but all too clearly, alas, it is an active willingness to be deceived.[6]

We have seen Teilhard's work referred to as being "false science," "undemonstrable scientifically," "theology-fiction," and "nonsense." But there were those who were favorable to Teilhard. Dobzhansky wrote:

An inspiring attempt to sketch an optimistic philosophy of the cosmic, biological, and human evolutions has been made by Teilhard de Chardin. . . . To modern man, so forlon and spiritually embattled in this vast and ostensibly meaningless universe, Teilhard de Chardin's evolutionary idea comes as a ray of hope. It fits the requirements of our time.[7]

But in his essay, "The Teilhardian Synthesis," Dobzhansky was more direct:

It would, then, be nearer the truth to say that Teilhard saw science illuminated by his mystical insights. . . . It is evidently the inspiration of a mystic, not a process of inference from scientific data, that lifts Teilhard to the heights of his eschatological vision.[8]

And he concluded that:

What made Teilhard's views novel and controversial was that he refused to pattern his thinking to fit it into any one of the recognized academic or intellectual categories. He was too much a scien-

---

[6]P. B. Medawar: Critical Notice: *The Phenomenon of Man. Mind*, 70:99, 106; 1961.

[7]Theodosius Dobzhansky: *Mankind Evolving: The Evolution of the Human Species.* New Haven, Yale University Press, 1962, pp. 347, 348.

[8]Theodosius Dobzhansky: *The Biology of Ultimate Concern.* New York, The New American Library, 1967, pp. 115, 137.

tist to set forth his conclusions in a manner wholly to please the theologians, and too much a theologian to make himself altogether a scientist. . . He defied those who regarded science and mystical vision no more blendable than oil and water. In an age of analysis he dared to essay a synthesis.[9]

Sir Julian Huxley had written a sympathetic "Introduction" to the English translation of *The Phenomenon of Man,* thus giving the work academic prestige. Huxley himself had been attempting an evolutionary synthesis, and therefore admired Teilhard's bold attempt:

The Phenomenon of Man is a very remarkable work by a very remarkable human being. . . . It is, if you like, visionary: but it is the product of a comprehensive and coherent vision. . . . In my view he achieved a remarkable success, and opened up vast territories of thought to further exploration and detailed mapping. . . . His influence on the world's thinking is bound to be important.[10]

Like Aristotle, Spinoza, Leibniz, and Hegel, Teilhard had desired to write a systematic view of man's place in the universe. But where they had merely been concerned with *development,* Teilhard saw the whole cosmos, including the human species, in *evolution.* And because he was a scientist, philosopher, theologian, mystic, and poet, his unique work is very difficult to evaluate.

Philosophical interpretations of evolution vary greatly. Ontologically, they may be monistic (materialistic or spiritualistic), dualistic, or pluralistic. Structurally, they may be mechanistic, vitalistic, finalistic, emergent, or cyclical. And finally, their orientation may be theistic, pantheistic, pantheistic, agnostic, or atheistic. Likewise, each position is historically and psychologically conditioned and therefore subject to future verification, modification, or falsification in light of further scientific knowledge. But ultimately, philosophies of evolution are variations of one of two major positions: materialism or spiritualism.

It will be evident that Teilhard's shortcomings are due to the theological and planetary orientation he needed to take for his

---

[9]Pierre Teilhard de Chardin: *Letters to Two Friends: 1926-1952.* New York, The New American Library, 1968, pp. 221, 222.

[10]Pierre Teilhard de Chardin: *The Phenomenon of Man.* New York, Harper and Row, 1965, pp. 11, 16, 21, 26.

bold but unsuccessful attempt to reconcile the universe and a personal God within an evolutionary panentheism.

A safe generalization is that Teilhard's Catholic philosophy of evolution rests upon four basic interrelated concepts: (a) spiritual monism or evolutionary panpsychism; (b) the "cosmic" Law of increasing centro-Complexity-Consciousness; (c) critical thresholds or levels or stages; (d) the Omega Point. The purpose of this monograph is threefold. First, to explicate Teilhard's four major assumptions as he developed them during years of reflection. Second, to compare and contrast these concepts with those positions held by previous philosophers of evolution, showing where Teilhard's assumptions have been anticipated to some extent in the evolutionary literature. Third, the author will critically examine these concepts and evaluate the significance of the Teilhardian synthesis from a naturalistic position.

Teilhard did not restrict himself to one method or field of inquiry. What we have is a natural theology in favor of spiritualism, vitalism, teleology, and Christianity. It must be reassessed in light of established facts and critical reflection.

The historical materialist can reinterpret Teilhard as Marx reinterpreted Hegel. From *this* orientation, the essential contribution of the works of Pierre Teilhard de Chardin is an evolutionary framework within which the future miscegenation, acculturation, and extraplanetary distribution of the human phylum is possible and intelligible.

Teilhard had written only three books: *The Divine Milieu* (1926-1927) ; *The Phenomenon of Man* (1938-1940) ; *Man's Place in Nature: The Human Zoological Group* (1949-1950). This investigation will refer to Teilhard's books, as well as the collections of his articles, essays, and letters. Relevant material in the evolutionary literature, both scientific and/or philosophical, will be referred to. It is hoped that this present work will aid in an understanding, appreciation, and critical evaluation of his work.

H. JAMES BIRX

ACKNOWLEDGMENTS

THE AUTHOR wishes to acknowledge his special indebtedness to Distinguished Professor Marvin Farber, without whose inspiration, guidance, and patience this task would not have been accomplished. This monograph is dedicated to him.

The author is also indebted to Drs. Dale M. Riepe, Lynn E. Rose, and Edward J. Buehler. They have always been encouraging and helpful.

The author would also like to express his deep appreciation for the inspiration and special attention given him by Dr. Aristotle Scoledes.

Finally, the writer takes this opportunity to thank Marcia Turley for her encouragement and help during the preparation of this manuscript. The author is indebted to June Licence for secretarial assistance.

H.J.B.

CONTENTS

PIERRE TEILHARD DE CHARDIN'S PHILOSOPHY OF EVOLUTION

Chapter I

TEILHARD'S LIFE AND WORK

Human inquiry is not free from value judgments, for scientists, philosophers, and theologians have vested interests. As such, no philosopher's system springs forth outside of his historico-social conditions. Teilhard's is no exception. To remove Teilhard and his synthesis from history is to do an injustice to his own evolutionary approach. Therefore, in order to understand the development of Teilhard's philosophy of evolution from his early World War I writings and first book *The Divine Milieu,* to his major synthetic work, *The Phenomenon of Man,* and the scientifically oriented *Man's Place in Nature: The Human Zoological Group,* it is necessary to consider the major events in his life that influenced the growth of his thought as recorded in his books, articles, essays, and letters.

On May 1, 1881, Marie-Joseph-Pierre Teilhard de Chardin was born at Sarcenat in the province of Auvergne, near Orcines and Clermont-Ferrand, France. He was the fourth of eleven children, and his ancestry could boast of Voltaire and Pascal. The influence of his mother, Berthe-Adèle de Dompierre d'Hornoy, kindled a deep, life-long concern for Christian mysticism, while his father, Emmanuel Teilhard de Chardin, encouraged devotion to natural history. Therefore, even as a child, Teilhard was interested in religion and science.

Teilhard had an irresistible need for some "One Thing Sufficient and Necessary," i.e. "Some One Essential Thing." As a result, his developing interests in astronomy, mineralogy, biology, and entomology were secondary to his striving toward an Absolute:

> And what used I to love? My genie of iron! With a plowhitch I
> believed myself, at seven years, rich with a treasure incorruptible,
> everlasting. And then it turned out that what I possessed was just a

bit of iron that rusted. At this discovery I threw myself on the lawn and shed the bitterest tears of my existence.[11]

Leaving his "most precious possessions," a collection of pebbles and rocks, Teilhard, at the age of eleven, entered the Jesuit secondary school of Notre-Dame de Mongré (1892). He studied Latin, Greek, German, and the sciences, and also developed an interest in philosophy. On March 20, 1899, he entered the Jesuit novitiate in Aix-en-Provence, for at the age of seventeen his desire to be "most perfect" determined his vocation to the Jesuits. As a junior, he continued his studies in philosophy and geology on the channel island of Jersey (1902-1905). After finishing his scholasticate in Jersey, Teilhard was sent to teach physics and chemistry in the Jesuit College of the Holy Family, Cairo, Egypt (1905-1908):

> I am to teach physics and chemistry to the classes corresponding here to third, humanities, rhetoric and philosophy. . . . I foresee that these years are going to be a valuable exercise in imagination for me.[12]

When free from teaching the natural and social sciences, which included botany, Teilhard preferred research in the deserts:

> I am becoming a supplier of shells, neuroptera, orthoptera, chrysalids, lepidoptera, etc., not to speak of making a fundamental study of geology, or rather, paleontology.[13]

Teilhard's first publication was an article, "A Week at Fayum" (1907), followed by his study on "The Eocene Strata of the Minieh Region" (1908). But despite his continued interests in geology and paleontology, Teilhard's religious views remained orthodox. He returned to Ore Place, the Jesuit house in Hastings on the Sussex coast, England, for his theological studies (1908-1912).

While remaining interested in geology, prehistory, botany, en-

---

[11]Claude Cuénot: *Teilhard de Chardin: A Biographical Study.* Baltimore, Helicon, 1965, p. 3. This work is the most comprehensive biographical study on Teilhard now available. See also, Robert Speaight: *Teilhard de Chardin: A Biography.* St. James's Place, London, Collins, 1967.

[12]Pierre Teilhard de Chardin: *Letters from Egypt: 1905-1908.* New York, Herder and Herder, 1965, pp. 28, 29.

[13]*Ibid.,* p. 115.

tomology, and ornithology, Teilhard's religious orientation was ever present:

> Theology makes me think about a lot of things and I'm beginning to perceive that there are so many other questions, less appealing, maybe, but more vital than the sciences, that I wonder if I shall not be side-tracked one day or another, unless they tell me not to do them, which is a strong possibility. . . . But I perceive that beside strictly scientific objects which have occupied my mind until now, there's a whole collection of human questions which constitute a field of studies just as lively no less fraught with problems. . . . It doesn't keep me from making a good wager that my first future destination will be to join a group of physical scientists.[14]

Teilhard was ordained priest on 24 August, 1911, in the chapel at Ore Place. The following year he successfully passed his final exam in theology, equivalent to the Doctorate in Theology. He then pursued his scientific researches at the Museum of Natural History in Paris under Marcellin Boule, Professor of Paleontology. He joined the Geological Society of France and established a life-long friendship with the prehistorian, the Abbé Henri Breuil.[15]

During this time, Teilhard had read Henri Bergson's *Creative Evolution* (1907). The work had a profound influence on Teilhard's thought. No longer able to hold to the orthodox Biblical account of *Genesis,* he adopted an evolutionary perspective. Within a scientific and religious framework, Teilhard now viewed the entire universe as an evolutionary process, referring to it as a cosmogenesis. But unlike Bergson, who saw evolution as a creative, vitalistic, and divergent process, Teilhard formulated a Catholic interpretation, stressing the convergent aspect of planetary evolution.

Bergsonian evolution had been founded upon an ontological dualism between matter and spirit or consciousness, i.e. the *élan vital.* The latter, Bergson held, is responsible for the irreversibility, continuity, and increasing creativity or novelty, complexity,

---

[14]Pierre Teilhard de Chardin: *Letters From Hastings: 1908-1912.* New York, Herder and Herder, 1968, p. 94.

[15]See Alan Houghton Broderick: *Father of Prehistory.* New York, Morrow, 1963.

diversity, and consciousness manifested in evolution. Teilhard, however, will adopt a monistic position giving a privileged position to spirit or consciousness. In short, we shall see that Teilhardian evolution is accumulative, irreversible, vitalistic, teleological, accelerating, personalizing, and converging or involuting toward greater improbabilities, complexity, consciousness, value, freedom, unity, equilibrium or synthesis, and perfection or being.

For Teilhard, the evolutionary doctrine had provided the necessary framework in which he could synthesize his interests in science, philosophy, and theology. It also could do justice to his cosmic interpretation of Christ and mystical temperament. He was already publicly advocating an evolutionary perspective:

> . . . I gave a lecture on the subject of evolution before the teaching staff of Notre Dame des Champs; I'm going to speak again on Tuesday about a related subject.[16]

Teilhard's first encounter with human paleontology (physical anthropology) was unfortunate. In 1909, he had met the amateur geologist, Charles Dawson. In 1912, joined by Professor Smith-Woodward, they visited Piltdown, England, where Dawson found a new fragment of a human skull and Teilhard found an elephant molar. The three returned to the same site in 1913, and Teilhard found the canine tooth from the jaw of the now infamous Piltdown Man or *Eoanthropus dawsoni*. The incident is significant, however, for it kindled an interest in human paleontology in the Jesuit-priest. And fortunately the cautious Teilhard remained skeptical of the skull fragments, as Piltdown Man presented a paleontological anomaly:

> In my opinion, all these reconstructions aren't of much interest and don't add any certainty about it; other pieces have to be found.[17]

In 1953, Dr. Kenneth P. Oakley, using the fluorine dating method, revealed that the specimen was fraudulent.[18] And Teilhard remarked: "Nothing seemed to 'fit' together. It's better that it all

---

[16]Pierre Teilhard de Chardin: *Letters From Paris: 1912-1914*. New York, Herder and Herder, 1967, p. 77.

[17]*Ibid.*, p. 99.

[18]See, J. S. Weiner: *The Piltdown Forgery*. New York, Oxford University Press, 1955.

fell through."[19] Nevertheless, Teilhard's future scientific research will take him to every major human paleontology site. In fact, the removal of Piltdown Man from the fossil evidence for human evolution favored Teilhard's own interpretation by supporting a continuous evolution of the human brain and culture. (Darwin had erroneously maintained that the "modern" cranial capacity had evolved *before* man became a tool-maker. We may now safely assume that man was a tool-maker over two million years ago with only a third of his present cranial capacity. In short, human intelligence and culture have evolved together in a dialectical relationship.)

In 1913, Teilhard joined the Abbé Breuil on an expedition to the prehistoric sites in the Pyrenees. Early mammalian fossils from Quercy and the Rheims area in the southwest of France provided the basis for his dissertation in geopaleontology. He worked on his thesis at the Institute of Human Paleontology at the Museum of Natural History, Paris:

> Right now I'm racking my brains trying to put the finishing touches on my thesis and trying to get it in order once and for all . . . but it's the illustrations for the thesis that are taking so long—not giving me time to do anything else on the side.[20]

Teilhard's work was interrupted when he was drafted in December, 1914, and assigned to the 13th division of the medical corps. He served at the front as a stretcher-bearer (1914-1919), and was cited three times, i.e. he was made Chevalier of the Légion d'Honneur, and held the Croix de Guerre and Médaille Militaire. He had shown great courage and humility, and his letters to his cousin Marguerite Teillhard-Chambon (Claude Aragonnès) illustrate his continued optimism and mysticism:

> The greatest sacrifice we can make, the greatest victory we can win over ourselves, is to surmount inertia, the tendency to follow the line of least resistance. . . . There's no doubt about it: the only man who knows (who experiences) right in the innermost depths of his being the weight and grandeur of war, is the man who goes over the top with bayonet and grenade. . . . The moralization

---

[19]Teilhard: *Letters From Paris: 1912-1914*, p. 10. Also see, Cuénot: *Teilhard de Chardin: A Biographical Study*, p .21.
[20]*Ibid.*, pp. 114, 119.

and sanctification of the Universe are the real progress, the real extension of the work which produce the brain and thought. . . . Isn't a priest a man who has to bear the burden of life in all its forms, and shows by his own life how human work and love of God can be combined?[21]

Fundamentally, I am experiencing with new intensity the intense joy and longing of clinging to God through everything. . . . True enough, my taste for the earth is strange, and, at first sight, most anti-Christian. But it's precisely because I feel so intensely this basic thing in the pagan soul that I feel in a strange position to speak advisedly (on equal terms) with those who worship the universe,— more certain, too, of the inter-relations and quasi-reconciliations possible between two positions I really believe to be to some degree united in me, and which in any case I certainly experience—a passion for the world, and a passion for God. . . . We have to remember that we are in process of becoming, and that all this multiplicity, through the charity which our Lord asks of us, in spite of our natural inclinations, will end by forming only one whole. . . . Yet should we not see God in the elements that make up this world, however contrary they may seem. . . . Only one thing matters, and should nourish our taste, our passion, for living: to feel that God is realized everywhere, in us and around us.[22]

Teilhard's experiences during the war did not deaden his spirit. On the contrary, he emerged more dedicated to the two objects of his passion: evolving nature and God. And his doctrine of converging evolution prevented him from adopting the tempting position of pantheism. For a mystical interpretation of a developing universe allowed for the future possibility of a union of a spiritualized cosmos or "matter" with a personal God, i.e. Teilhard had replaced pantheism with a process panentheism. He focused on this position, and dedicated his life to scientifically demonstrating and philosophically clarifying its validity and necessity for human survival. For this theological perspective and inspiration, he relied heavily upon the writings of St. Paul and St. John to substantiate the Catholic orthodoxy of his cosmic and mystical "vision."

After the war, and with renewed strength and hope in the fu-

---

[21]Pierre Teilhard de Chardin: *The Making of a Mind: Letters From a Soldier-Priest, 1914-1919.* New York, Harper and Row, 1965, pp. 58, 72, 166, 183.

[22]*Ibid.*, pp. 141, 165, 202, 210, 249.

ture progress of mankind, Teilhard took his solemn vows on 26 May, 1918, at Sainte-Foy-Les-Lon, France. His early writings during the war had been primarily concerned with the immanence or pan-Christism and transcendence of God, and the converging evolution of spirit toward a creative union with the Absolute through love. But the Jesuit-priest now returned to scientific research. He taught as Associate Professor of Geology at the Institut Catholique (1920-1923) while resuming work on his doctoral thesis on the mammifers of the Lower Eocene in France, and the layers of soil in which they were found. However, his religious dedication remained:

> I'm emerging, as I told you, from these four and a half years of retreat, with a store of fresh energies and a precise Christian ideal, which I am anxious to test and use. . . . What keeps me calm is my complete confidence that if there is a real ray of light in "my gospel", somehow or other that ray will shine forth. . . . With God's help, I must live my "vision" fully, logically, and without deviation. There's nothing more infectious than the example of a life governed by conviction and principle. And now I feel sufficiently drawn to and equipped for, such a life.[23]

And in his correspondence to the philosopher Auguste Valensin, Teilhard wrote:

> Just as spirit appeared in man by making some sort of use of the rudimentary forms of instinct, the supernatural is continuously being formed by the super-creation of our nature. . . . But quite apart from that, if we had to wait for mystical unification with Christ before we addressed ourselves to the world, we would probably never begin our human effort.[24]

In 1922, Teilhard received the title of doctor with distinction at the Sorbonne for his thesis on "The Mammals of the Lower Eocene Period in France."

A fellow-Jesuit, Père Emile Licent, had built a museum and laboratory at Tientsin, China. Its purpose was the study of Chinese geology, mineralogy, paleontology, and botany. As director of the project, Licent asked Teilhard to join the "French Paleon-

---

[23]*Ibid.*, pp. 251, 269, 286.

[24]Henri de Lubac (Ed.): *Correspondence.* New York, Herder and Herder, 1967, pp. 33, 50.

tological Mission." And on 6 April, 1923, Teilhard left for Tient-sin. In his letters to the Abbé Breuil, he revealed his first impressions:

> My strongest impression at the moment is a confused one that the human world (to look no further than that) is a huge and disparate thing, just about as coherent, at the moment, as the surface of a rough sea. I still believe, for reasons imbued with mysticism and metaphysics, that this incoherence is the prelude to a unification. . . . Today what counts for me (as for you) is the future of things; whereas here I am plunged into the past. . . . However, mysticism remains the great science and the great art, the only power capable of synthesising the riches accumulated by other forms of human activity.[25]

And from Tientsin, Teilhard wrote the following to Leontine Zanta:

> I am more and more persuaded that this dilemma confronts us: either the world is moving towards some universal absolute (in which case it can go on living and progressing), or else such an end doesn't exist (in which case the universe is manifestly *unable to nourish the life it has produced* ever since this life became capable of reflexion and criticism; it is unbreathable and abortive).[26]

Teilhard accompanied Licent on an expedition to inner Mongolia and the Ordos desert. It was during this expedition into the Ordos desert that, on Easter Sunday, having no means to celebrate Mass on the feast of the Transfiguration, Teilhard finished his philosophical and mystical poem, "The Mass on the World" (1923):

> . . . I, your priest, will make the whole earth my altar and on it will offer you all the labours and sufferings of the world. . . . Receive, O Lord, this all-embracing host which your whole creation, moved by your magnetism, offers you at this dawn of a new day. . . . You know how your creatures can come into being only, like shoot from stem, as part of an endlessly renewed process of evolution. . . . Like the monist I plunge into the all-inclusive One; but the One is so perfect that as it receives me and I lose myself in it I can

[25]Pierre Teilhard de Chardin: *Letters From a Traveller.* New York, Harper and Brothers, 1962, pp. 73, 81, 86-87.

[26]Pierre Teilhard de Chardin: *Letters to Leontine Zanta.* New York, Harper and Row, 1969, p. 49.

find in it the ultimate perfection of my own individuality. . . .
All of us, inescapably, exist in you, the universal *milieu* in which
and through which all things live and have their being. . . . For me,
my God, all joy and all achievement, the very purpose of my being
and all my love of life, all depend on this one basic vision of the
union between yourself and the universe.[27]

(We shall see that for Teilhard converging evolution or cosmogenesis will allow for the universe and Christ to become one within a Christogenesis which will reach its fulfillment in a union
with God.)

On 13 September, 1924, Teilhard left China and returned to
France. During the winter of 1925-1926 he gave four lectures on
evolution, and developed his concept of the noosphere. (The
noosphere represented human evolution or hominization when
viewed from a planetary perspective and considered biologically,
psychologically, and technologically. But spiritually, the noosphere represented the accumulation of persons or reflective monads or centers-of-consciousness within a planetary layer or envelope. Through evolution, Teilhard held that these reflective monads were converging or involuting toward God.)

Now because of Teilhard's evolutionary orientation and his
unorthodox view of Original Sin, his Jesuit superiors felt compelled to withdraw him from the Institut Catholique. (His lectures were challenging the traditional Catholic view of a static
planet with an hierarchy of eternally fixed forms.) Likewise, he
was confined to scientific research (i.e. descriptive geology and
paleontology), forbidden to teach or publish on philosophy and
theology, and exiled back to China in 1926.

Back at Tientsin, Teilhard wrote his first book, *The Divine
Milieu* (November 1926—March 1927). It was a spiritual essay on
life or the inward vision, and attempted to reconcile a love of
nature with the love of God. It advocated the divinization of activities and passivities, and supported the doctrine of evolution:

We may, perhaps, imagine that the creation was finished long ago.

---

[27]Pierre Teilhard de Chardin: *Hymn of the Universe.* New York, Harper and
Row, 1965, pp. 19, 20, 22, 26, 35, 36.

But that would be quite wrong. It continues still more magnificently, and at the highest levels of the world.[28]

Critical of Christian asceticism, Teilhard taught that the goal of human evolution would be reached only through collective human effort:

> Why separate and contrast the two natural phases of a single effort? Your essential duty and desire is to be united with God.[29]

Like Bonaventure (1217-1274), Duns Scotus (1266-1308), and Cusa (1401-1464), Teilhard's philosophy of evolution is Christocentric. His panentheistic orientation (i.e. the belief that God is at once both immanent and transcendent) is evident:

> God reveals himself everywhere, beneath our groping efforts, as a universal milieu, only because he is the ultimate point upon which all realities converge. . . . However vast the divine milieu may be, it is in reality a centre . . . the ultra-vital, the ultra-sensitive, the ultra-active point of the universe. . . . Our divine milieu is at the antipodes of false pantheism . . . The divine milieu, although it may still enfold us, exists only incompletely, or not at all, for us. . . . The divine milieu which will ultimately be one in the Pleroma, must begin to become one during the earthly phase of our existence.[30]

For Teilhard, "material" evolution was spiritualizing itself and therefore purifying itself. Cosmic evolution, which at first reveals itself as a multiplicity of evolutions, is actually the unfolding of one single great mystery through the immanent force of Christ.

Teilhard's position is expressed briefly in his basic syllogism:

> At the heart of our existence, each soul exists
> for God, in our Lord.

> But all reality, even material reality, around
> each one of us, exists for our souls.

> Hence, all sensible reality, around each one of
> us, exists, through our souls, for God in our
> Lord.[31]

---

[28]Pierre Teilhard de Chardin: *The Divine Milieu.* New York, Harper and Row, 1968, p. 62.

[29]*Ibid.,* p. 95.

[30]*Ibid.,* pp. 114, 115, 116, 118, 143.

[31]*Ibid.,* p. 56.

Teilhard was convinced that through collective effort a new earth is being slowly engendered. And as a result of directional evolution, the Second Coming of Christ, the Parousia, would result in the union of a collective mankind with a personal God, forming the Pleroma:

> . . . in which the substantial *one* and the created *many* fuse without confusion in a *whole* which, without adding anything essential to God, will nevertheless be a sort of triumph and generalization of being.[32]

In short, the Pleroma consists of the union of mankind with God, an event brought about through the fulfillment of an evolving, cosmic Christ. It is evident that Teilhard's position rests upon faith. Yet it is not surprising that he was refused publication of his first book.

Nevertheless, Teilhard continued to see Christ in "matter," and God in evolution. He was never to abandon this position, but would later attempt to give it scientific justification in his second book, *The Phenomenon of Man.*

In a letter to a friend, Teilhard revealed his continued effort at synthesis:

> I can no longer touch Christ (the true, the great) in myself except in the world. Therefore the two must glorify one another mutually in me. . . . Those who do not hear the fundamental harmony of the Universe which I try to transcribe (fortunately, many do) look in what I write for some kind of narrowly logical system, and are confused or angry. Fundamentally, it is not possible to transmit directly by words the perception of a quality, a taste. Once again, it would be more to my purpose to be a shadow of Wagner than a shadow of Darwin. Taking myself as I am, I see no better course than to strive by all means to reveal Humanity to Man.[33]

In 1929, Teilhard was appointed scientific advisor to the National Chinese Geological Survey as well as Advisor and Collab-

---

[32]*Ibid.*, p. 122.

[33]Pierre Teilhard de Chardin: *Letters to Two Friends: 1926-1952.* New York, The New American Library, 1968, pp. 25, 59. In fact, Teilhard's *The Phenomenon of Man* does resemble a Wagnerian opera. They are both symbolic, mystical, poetic, and exalt human love and progress. Concerning Wagner, the author is thinking particularly of *Der Ring des Nibelungen* (1876) and *Parsifal* (1882). It is not surprising that *Parsifal* was Teilhard's favorite Wagnerian music drama.

orator of the Cenozoic Research Laboratory established by Dr. Davidson Black,[34] then Director of the Peking Union Medical School. He also joined the Central Mongolian Expedition (1930) and the Yellow Expedition (Citroën trans-Asia mission or the Croisière Jaune) into Central Asia (1931-1932). During his twenty years in China, he would leave to take part in geological and paleontological field trips to India, Burma, Java, Ethiopia, and the United States. (Scientifically, Teilhard was primarily a geologist, secondly a paleontologist specializing in mammals, and only thirdly a prehistorian and anthropologist, favoring physical anthropology.)

It is ironic that Teilhard was relocated in China because of his evolutionary orientation. For only twenty miles southwest of Peking is Chou-Kou-Tien, an area which was soon to become and remain one of the world's most significant human paleontological sites.

In 1929, the largest part of the cerebral cranium of a hominid was unearthed at Chou-Kou-Tien. Teilhard received worldwide recognition for his scientific articles which popularized the series of findings at the site. Yet Teilhard neither discovered the fossil remains nor analyzed them. However, he contributed to an understanding of the geological and paleontological features of the site. And he was always aware of the philosophical and theological implications of the findings.

In 1928, fossil remains of the jawbone of a hominid had been found. These and the cranium were held to belong to Peking Man, *Sinanthropus pekinensis*. Teilhard wrote:

> *Sinanthropus* fortunately helps us to understand through what successive forms the human type took shape among the rest of life. . . . Sinanthropus, more man than Pithecanthropus, is nevertheless very different from and more primitive than Neanderthal man. . . . It seems perhaps wisest in the present state of researches to regard Peking man as a being in whom the fire of thought was already alight and had no doubt been so for a long time—as already *Homo*

---

[34]See Dora Hood: *Davidson Black: A Biography.* Toronto, University of Toronto Press, 1964. After the untimely death of Davidson Black in 1934, Teilhard was made temporary Director of the Peking Union Medical School until the arrival of Black's replacement, Dr. Franz Weidenreich.

faber, walking upright and using his hands as we do. . . . Already *Homo faber,* he was certainly also (at least as far as his mental powers are concerned) *Homo sapiens.*[35]

The discovery of the *Sinanthropus* material (1928-1934) reinforced Teilhard's evolutionary perspective and gave human evolution the needed scientific grounding. For Teilhard not only was evolution applicable to geology and biology in general, but also and more importantly to the origin and development of man and his culture in particular. (Was not the entire universe and everything in it involved in a cosmogenesis?)

Teilhard's knowledge of the *Sinanthropus* material was supplemented by field trips to Central Asia with George Barbour (1934), to India and then Burma with Helmut de Terra (1935, 1937-1938), and to Java to investigate the Pithecanthropoid material at the invitations of G. H. R. von Koenigswald (1935, 1938). During the Yangtze Expedition into Central Asia, George Barbour noted that Teilhard:

> . . . was clearly trying to draw together into a new perspective ideas from a wide range of sources which might give him a fresh outlook on the problems of science and religion.[36]

And Helmut de Terra also recorded his impressions:

> He had a brilliant capacity for proceeding straight to a synthesis from carefully sifted details. . . . His impatience was that of a scientist obsessed with spiritual questions and eager to grasp the underlying meaning of history. . . . In his company, one could always bank on a mental reflex which placed facts in a wider context and seemed to correlate them with Platonic "ideas". . . . He had a natural faculty for endowing detailed work with greater meaning. . . . Let no one cherish any false illusions about the thoroughness of Teilhard's scientific research. . . . Teilhard was a unique blend of personal revelation and scientific experience . . . a scientist who loved mankind and took a deliberate interest in its evolution.[37]

---

[35]Pierre Teilhard de Chardin: *The Appearance of Man.* New York, Harper and Row, 1965, pp. 67, 70, 91, 102.

[36]George B. Barbour: *In the Field with Teilhard de Chardin.* New York, Herder and Herder, 1965, pp. 37-38.

[37]Helmut de Terra: *Memories of Teilhard de Chardin.* New York, Harper and Row, 1964, pp. 24, 29, 67, 72, 89, 121, 141.

In a letter, Teilhard had recorded his own reaction to these trips:

> In brief, both in India with de Terra and in Java with Koenigswald, I pitched most opportunely on two of the hottest sectors in the prehistory front—and just at the very moment to take part in decisive offensives. This is proving a great addition to my experience and another valuable plank in my platform. But fundamentally it gives me only moderate satisfaction. As a purpose in life, my science (to which I owe so much) seems to me to be less and less worthwhile. For a long time now, my chief interest in life has lain in some sort of effort towards a plainer disclosing of God in the world. It's a more killing task but it's my only true vocation and nothing can turn me from it.[38]

He had also expressed the same feeling in a letter to another friend:

> I owe the best of myself to geology, but everything it has taught me tends to turn me away from dead things. . . . Without geology I would have understood nothing of the World, and now that I think I have understood the World, I want to work more directly from the *living* thing. . . . It is the extensions of the Universe into the Human that fascinate me. . . . There is only one foe against whom I should fully like to give my life: immobility.[39]

In 1937, after years of scientific research and rigorous reflection, Teilhard started preliminary notes on his synthesis. The work progressed steadily, with Teilhard writing one or two paragraphs each day. Finally, after two years, he completed his major book, *The Phenomenon of Man* (June 1938—June 1940). In September he wrote to George Barbour from the shortlived Institute of Geo-Biology in Peking:

> Aside from geological and paleontological studies under way, I have been able to finish up a book on Man—half scientific, half philosophical—into which I have put the gist of the ideas closest to my heart. I hope its publication will not run into trouble from my Order. However, as things stand, I do not see how to get the needed authorization to print.[40]

---

[38]*Letters From a Traveller*, pp. 218-219.
[39]*Letters to Two Friends*, pp. 88, 89, 91, 136.
[40]Barbour: *In the Field with Teilhard de Chardin*, p. 110.

And on 6 August, 1944, Teilhard learned that ecclesiastical permission to publish *The Phenomenon of Man* had been refused.

Teilhard remained in Peking during World War II. Then in 1946, he left for France and was never to return to China. And although he suffered his first heart attack in 1947, the following year he went himself to Rome to seek publication of *The Divine Milieu* and *The Phenomenon of Man* (which he had slightly altered), as well as to obtain permission to succeed the late Abbé Breuil as Professor at the College de France. Unfortunately, all of Teilhard's requests were refused.

Discouraged but still optimistic, Teilhard wrote his third book, *Man's Place in Nature: The Human Zoological Group* (1949). Although it was a clearer, more scientific restatement of *The Phenomenon of Man,* it was not published during his life. However, he continued to express his thoughts in correspondence and essays circulated among his friends. And he was elected to the Academie des Sciences (Institut de France).

In 1951, Teilhard made his seventh visit to New York City where he accepted a research post at the Wenner-Gren Foundation for Anthropological Research (Viking Foundation). And at the invitation of C. Van Riet Lowe, the foundation sponsored Teilhard's two visits to the Australopithecinae sites in South Africa (1951, 1953). (During his life, he had investigated the major Australopithecinae, Pithecanthropoid, and Neanderthaloid sites.)

Teilhard had expressed a wish to die on the Feast of the Resurrection. And at the age of seventy-four, he died of a sudden stroke on 10 April, 1955, in New York City. His death had occurred, with a certain macabre appropriateness, on Easter Sunday evening. He was buried at Saint Andrew on the Hudson, in the cemetery of the Jesuit novitiate for the New York Province. Fortunately, Teilhard had entrusted his unpublished manuscripts to the care of a friend, Jeanne Mortier. And by the fall of 1955, a French edition of his *The Phenomenon of Man* was published. (Teilhard's complete bibliography amounts to over five hundred titles.)

The Phenomenon of Man is a remarkable synthesis of science, philosophy, religion, and mysticism within a Catholic interpretation of evolution. In its "Preface," Teilhard wrote that he is offering a "scientific treatise" dealing with the *whole* phenomenon of man, i.e. an introduction to an explanation of man's place in the cosmos *solely* as a phenomenon:

> If this book is to be properly understood, it must be read not as a work on metaphysics, still less as a sort of theological essay, but purely and simply as a scientific treatise.[41]

Yet the book abounds with assumptive reasoning and is, as we shall see, ultimately grounded in theology and mysticism. Why, then, did Teilhard claim that it was a scientific treatise? First, he had wanted to gain the attention of the scientific world. And second, he held that his "vision" was, at least to a convincing degree, scientifically demonstrable. The work contained two basic assumptions:

> The first is the primacy accorded to the psychic and to thought in the stuff of the universe, and the second is the "biological" value attributed to the social fact around us.[42]

In the "Foreword: Seeing," Teilhard held that either we adequately *see* man's place within the framework of phenomenon and appearance (and therefore understand his evolutionary position or essence and destination) or mankind shall perish. With the use of the seven categories or "senses" of space, time, quantity (number), quality (novelty), proportion, motion, and organism (unity) to illuminate our vision, Teilhard taught that the result of a "scientific" investigation of man's place in nature will reveal that man is the spiritual and structural center of the physical universe. His anthropocentrism is unequivocable:

> The true physics is that which will, one day, achieve the inclusion of man in his wholeness in a coherent picture of the world. . . . In such a vision man is seen not as a static centre of the world—as he for long believed himself to be—but as the axis and leading shoot of evolution, which is something much finer.[43]

---

[41]*The Phenomenon of Man*, p. 29.

[42]*Ibid.*, p. 30.

[43]*Ibid.*, p. 36. Teilhard never developed an epistemology. He relied upon religiously oriented assumptions and mystical intuitions to synthesize scientific data.

Within an evolutionary framework, Teilhard saw the continuity of three fundamentally unique events: the emergence of Pre-Life, Life, and Thought. And he gave Thought a privileged position in the universe. For his purpose was to supplement the previous analytical studies of the external, structural evolution of matter with a complementary historico-phenomenological analysis of the internal, converging evolution of consciousness or spirit. He neither claimed to have given a final explanation of things nor of having constructed a metaphysical system as Leibniz had done.

In the last analysis, Teilhard's *The Phenomenon of Man* is a largely tentative, personal, suggestive but incomplete essay founded upon a mystical presupposition:

> Fuller being is closer union: such is the kernel and conclusion of this book.[44]

Now let us consider each of Teilhard's four fundamental, interrelated assumptions which give coherency to his evolutionary system: (a) Evolutionary Monism, (b) Law of Complexity-Consciousness, (c) Critical Thresholds, (d) Omega Point.

---

[44]*Ibid.*, p. 31.

Chapter II

TEILHARD'S EVOLUTIONARY MONISM

Teilhard's Catholic philosophy of evolution rests upon an ontological monism. As a result of giving a privileged position to mind or consciousness, Teilhard held that the universe is ultimately spiritual or psychic in nature and developing toward greater perfection and unity. His position of evolutionary panpsychism or objective idealism is religious in orientation, and is more implicit than explicit in his writings.

A. THE DEVELOPMENT OF TEILHARD'S SPIRITUALISM

Teilhard desired to take account of the significance and purpose of consciousness in the universe. He started from an objective and subjective consideration of man as a biological, social, and spiritual event in nature, and extrapolated the necessary conditions of the universe to bring the human phylum into existence and guarantee its fulfillment. In an early essay, "Cosmic Life" (1916), he presented an embryonic form of his intellectual testament:

> First there is *the revelation of the unique matter,* and then, even more wonderful, *that of the unique soul.* . . . The truth about the way in which things are constituted is this: *Everything that exists has a basis of thought,* not a basis of ether. Necessarily, then, consciousness has everywhere the power to re-emerge, because everywhere it is consciousness, dormant or ossified *that persists.*[1]

Although Teilhard had adopted a position of panpsychism, he retained an unclear distinction between "matter" and spirit. However, what *is* clear is that he held cosmic evolution to be a spiritualizing process. In "The Mystical Milieu" (1917), he committed himself to monism. He held that "there is but a single

---

[1] Pierre Teilhard de Chardin: *Writings in Time of War.* New York, Harper and Row, 1968, pp. 25, 40-41.

matter created to maintain the successive growths of consicousness in the cosmos. . . . ."[2]

In "Creative Union" (1917), Teilhard sounded very much like Leibniz (however, Leibniz was neither an evolutionist nor held to a converging, finalistic structure of the universe) :

It is refinement of psychism that determines the true, absolute, position of the monads in the ascending series of beings. . . . Soul, at all its degrees, was born of this progressive concentration of the primordial dust.[3]

In "The Eternal Feminine" (1918), Teilhard taught that "matter is a tendency, a direction—it is the side of Spirit that we meet as we fall back."[4] He never doubted the spiritual evolution or ultimate unity of the entire universe. (Both "matter" and plurality were merely temporal phenomena.) And in "The Universal Element" (1919), he wrote:

. . . strictly speaking, there is in the universe only one single individual (one single monad), that of the whole (conceived in its organized plurality) .[5]

These early essays, written during Teilhard's involvement in World War I, depict a religious mind struggling to reconcile the material world of the naturalists with the spiritual orientation of the theologians. (Teilhard even recorded his mystical experiences.) [6]

Unlike Descartes, whose subjective methodology unfortunately reinstated into the history of philosophy an ontological dualism between mind and extension or matter (in fact, Descartes held that there were three separate substances: mind, extension or matter, and God), Teilhard continued to develop his monistic metaphysics. It is evident that his thoughts were moving in the direction of spiritual monism. In "Science and Christ: Or Analysis and Synthesis" (1921), he wrote that:

Materialism is born from a fundamental error of perspective. . . .

---

[2]*Ibid.*, p. 121.
[3]*Ibid.*, pp. 154, 155.
[4]*Ibid.*, p. 195.
[5]*Ibid.*, pp. 296-297.
[6]*Hymn of the Universe*, pp. 41-55.

To the informed observer, analysis of matter reveals the priority and primacy of Spirit.[7]

And in "My Universe" (1924), Teilhard gives a clear summary of his theistic and spiritualistic orientation:

Every unity of the world, provided it be a natural unity, is a monad. . . . In the system of creative union, moreover, it becomes impossible to continue crudely to contrast Spirit and matter. . . . Matter and Spirit are not opposed as two separate things, as two natures, but as two directions of evolution within the world. . . . There is ultimately one single physical reality developing in the cosmos, one single monad. . . . Within the cosmos all the elements are dependent upon one another ontologically, in the ascending order of their true being (which means of their consciousness); and the entire cosmos, as one complete whole, is held up, "informed," by the powerful energy of a higher, and unique, Monad which gives to everything below itself its definitive intelligibility and its definitive power of action and reaction.[8]

We shall see later that this unique Monad which is responsible for the evolution and unity of the universe is the Christian God.

Teilhard will maintain that the order of interacting monads is not a continuum, but manifests significant levels differing in *kind*. Each successive level of monads is held to be more perfect than the lower levels, i.e. more conscious or more God-like (like Leibniz's monads, each element of the universe mirrors God imperfectly). Leibniz had held to an unbroken series of an infinite number of developing monads, each mirroring the Absolute Monad by degree (no two monads could ever be psychically identical). Like Leibniz, Teilhard also held that God is responsible for the order in monadic development. But Leibniz's monads did not interact, although he held the process to be teleological and eternal. Unlike Leibniz, Teilhard will assume a Christian end to planetary evolution.

In his first essay entitled "The Phenomenon of Man" (1928), Teilhard emphasized that sidereal evolution is not only spiritual but *irreversible:*

---

[7]Pierre Teilhard de Chardin: *Science and Christ.* New York, Harper and Row, 1965, pp. 28, 31.

[8]*Ibid.*, pp. 47, 51, 52, 57.

However far back we may trace it, the phenomenon of consciousness seems to have been becoming more generalised on earth and more marked.[9]

During his years in China, free from teaching responsibilities and public appearances, Teilhard had time to reflect upon his scientific research and the *implications* of evolution from a Christian perspective. And although immersed in geological and paleontological investigations, his preoccupation with "matter" did not divert his primary concern for the spiritual fulfillment of the human species. His participation in the *Sinanthropus* excavations and field trips to other major primate sites in India and Java reinforced his view that man is the most recent product of an organic evolution that has its origin billions of years in the past. Man's existence on earth, although covering a span of several millions of years, represented nevertheless a unique cosmic event. Through the emergence of man, the spiritual universe had become self-conscious. And becoming less concerned with the origin and development of the human phylum, Teilhard now concentrated on providing a system with a suitable outcome for the future spiritualization and convergence of a collective mankind. (In his popularizations of the *Sinanthropus* finds, he had and could only hint at the theological implications he was deriving from the design he had held to be manifested in planetary evolution.)

Teilhard wrote philosophical and theological essays, hoping that someday his superiors would grant the necessary permission needed to see them in print. And there was always present the desire to write a book in which he would synthesize science, philosophy, and theology to give a proper account of the significance of man's place in the world. In his first book, *The Divine Milieu* (1927), Teilhard held that:

Matter is the common, universal, tangible setting, infinitely shifting and varied, in which we live. . . . The frontier between spiritual matter and carnal matter is constantly moving upward. . . . This is the *general "drift" of matter towards spirit*.[10]

And in "Man's Place in Nature" (1932), he concluded:

---

[9]*Ibid.*, p. 94.
[10]*The Divine Milieu*, pp. 107, 109, 110.

A consciousness gradually waking by way of countless fumblings, this would, in this case, be the essential picture of evolution.[11]

Teilhard held that the existence of a cosmic development of Spirit was the greatest discovery made by modern science, as it implied that man is:

> . . . nothing more or less than that portion of the Weltstoff that has emerged into consciousness of self. . . . The personal is the highest state in which we are able to apprehend the stuff of the universe.[12]

He argued that since man is the end product of cosmic evolution, and since the essence of man is that he is a *person,* then the evolutionary universe is therefore ultimately a personalizing process. (Continuing this argument, he will later assume that planetary evolution will terminate in the formation of a Supreme Person.)

Teilhard's clearest position on the nature of the stuff of the universe is presented in his major work, *The Phenomenon of Man.* Plurality, unity, and energy are held to be the three basic characteristics of the universe, i.e. the boundless cosmos as a whole is represented as manifesting a *system,* a *totum,* and a *quantum* respectively. Matter is ultimately composed of homogeneous units of energy that are infinitesimal, dynamic, and interdependent:

> This fundamental discovery that all bodies owe their origin to arrangements of a single initial corpuscular type is the beacon that lights the history of the universe to our eyes.[13]

And these units of "matter" or energy reveal themselves in an indefinite development within duration or a converging space-time continuum:

> In this new perspective the world appears like a mass in process of

---

[11]Pierre Teilhard de Chardin: *The Vision of the Past.* New York, Harper and Row, 1966, p. 181.

[12]*Science and Christ,* pp. 132, 136.

[13]*The Phenomenon of Man,* p. 48. Teilhard's atomistic position reminds us of the seeds of Anaxagorous, the atoms of Leucippus, Democritus, and Lucretius, and the monads of Bruno and Leibniz. It may also be noted that although Teilhard sometimes refers to the universe as being boundless, we are safe in assuming that he actually held it to be finite, although of indeterminate size.

transformation. . . . Matter reveals itself to us *in a state of genesis or becoming.*[14]

For Teilhard, energy evolves from a homogeneous base to a future limit, i.e. "a superior pole to the world—the *omega point.*"[15] Structurally, he held that the evolution of energy represents a cone, spiral, or pyramid. That the Omega Point represents the apex of this structure, and therefore the goal of evolution, will be dealt with in Chapter V. However, this spiral structure of evolution is absolutely crucial to Teilhard's cosmological model and should always be kept in mind by the reader.

Teilhard is considering the ontological status of a cosmic embryogenesis through which the potentialities of the universe are being actualized within a space-time continuum.[16] He held that the system is closed and self-sufficient, there being no addition of external energy to replace the energy irrecoverably "entropised" as the cost of creative, evolutionary syntheses. In short, cosmogenesis is subject to the two principles of the Conservation and Dissipation of Energy. However, Teilhard also held that the evolution of energy is in a direction antithetical to cosmic entropy, i.e. while the *physical* energy of the universe is dissipating to a state of static equilibrium, the *psychical* energy of the universe is evolving and collecting, and will eventually converge or involute upon God at the Omega Point.

But what is the ultimate nature of this cosmic energy? Is Teilhard's final ontological interpretation of evolution materialistic, spiritualistic, or dualistic? At first, Teilhard attempted to unite the positions of materialism and spiritualism by merely making a distinction between determined *tangential* energy (the Without of things, i.e. the level-oriented physical or horizontal component of evolution) and free *radial* energy (the Within of things, i.e. the dynamic or vitalistic mental or vertical component of evolu-

---

[14]*Ibid.,* pp. 47, 49.

[15]*Ibid.,* p. 66.

[16]Teilhard wrote, *"In the world, nothing could ever burst forth as final across the different thresholds successively traversed by evolution (however critical they be) which has not already existed in an obscure and primordial way." Ibid.,* p. 71. And, "Nothing can enter into the universe that does not emerge from it." *Science and Christ,* p. 60.

tion). The two forms of energy are interrelated so that every-thing in the universe appears to have a physical and a psychical aspect:

> Since the stuff of the universe has an inner aspect at one point of itself, there is necessarily a double aspect to its structure, that is to say in every region of space and time—in the same way, for instance, as it is granular: co-extensive with their Without, there is a Within to things.[17]

In short, *radial* energy or *consciousness* or *spontaneity* is:

> . . . a cosmic extension, and as such is surrounded by an aura of indefinite spatial and temporal extension. . . . This "interior" should obtrude itself as existing everywhere in nature from all time.[18]

Teilhard held that while scientists were concerned only with the structure of matter and the Marxists with historicoeconomic determinism, they both failed to do justice to the significance and historical emergence of consciousness. Likewise, he held that the phenomenologists and existentialists had not taken the doctrine and implications of evolution seriously, while the naturalists did not appreciate the significance of Christianity for human survival. Teilhard's own approach is a bold and unique attempt to do justice to physical and psychical evolution.

Thus far, Teilhard's position rests upon three observations:

1. *Atomicity is a common property of the Within and the Without of things.*
2. *Refracted rearwards along the course of evolution, consciousness displays itself qualitatively as a spectrum of shifting shades whose lower terms are lost in the night.*
3. *Spiritual perfection (or conscious "centreity") and material synthesis (or complexity) are but the two aspects or connected parts of one and the same phenomenon.*[19]

But Teilhard does not retain the distinction between *radial* and *tangential* energy when he leaves the phenomenal level of investigation to consider the ultimate ontology of the universe. In a crucial passage in *The Phenomenon of Man*, he not only

---

[17]*The Phenomenon of Man*, p. 56.
[18]*Ibid.*
[19]*Ibid.*, pp. 59, 60, 61.

gives *radial* energy a privileged position but commits himself to a spiritual monism or objective idealism:

> In the last analysis, *somehow or other*, there must be a single energy operating in the world. . . . We shall assume that, essentially, all energy is psychic in nature.[20]

This fundamental and crucial aspect of Teilhard's philosophy of evolution has surprisingly been largely overlooked or misrepresented. Teilhard himself continues to refer to "matter" in his later writings while equating progress with the growth of consciousness. But the author believes that this ambiguity can be resolved by making the philosophical distinction between appearance and reality, i.e. the distinction between epistemology and ontology. From the epistemological perspective, one may distinguish between matter, i.e. that which appears within human experience and is referred to as matter, and one's own personality or mind or mental activity. In contrast, however, one may wish to assume that ontologically all of reality is spiritual or mental in nature. (A crucial distinction is called for between objective and subjective methodologies and the actual status of the concrete reality.) Forms of spiritual ontologies have been advocated by recent idealists, e.g. Leibniz, Kant, and Hegel. The author believes that Teilhard's position must be viewed as supporting objective idealism if it is to be at all intelligible.

It is worth noting that Teilhard's evolutionary form of objective idealism prevented him from adopting both a Berkeleyan form of idealism or the Husserlian "problem" of intersubjectivity (the result of the overextension of a subjective methodology) or solipsism. This is because he held that the beginning of cosmogenesis was prior to and independent of human experience, i.e. self-consciousness:

> So vast are the dimensions of the universe disclosed by the present that, for this reason alone, all sorts of things must have happened in it before man was there to witness them. Long before the awaken-

---

[20]*Ibid.*, pp. 63, 64. In the first English translation of *The Phenomenon of Man* (1959), this one fundamental energy had been mistranslated as being "physical" rather than "psychical" in nature. This unfortunate error has been responsible for many misrepresentations of Teilhard's ontological position.

ing of thought on earth, manifestations of cosmic energy must have been produced which have no parallel today.[21]
For the process to be *seen* as it really is, we should require a terrestrial witness simultaneously present through the whole of duration, and the very idea is monstrous.[22]

Reacting rightly against a crude form of mechanistic materialism, Teilhard adopted a form of organism. But his interpretation of nature is also vitalistic:

Beneath the "tangential" we find the "radial." The impetus of the world, glimpsed in the great drive of consciousness, can only have its ultimate source in some *inner* principle, which alone could explain its irreversible advance towards higher psychisms.[23]

Teilhard held that philosophically consciousness causes the further evolution of itself. Theologically, he held that God is both immanent and transcendent (a position of panentheism). The immanent nature of God is manifested as *radial* or spiritual energy or Becoming, while the transcendent nature of God is the Supreme Center of Love or Being. By equating God's immanent nature with a cosmic interpretation of the Christ, Teilhard held that Christ's presence in "matter" allows God to make things make themselves. In short, vitalism and teleology are crucial elements in his process philosophy. Cosmic evolution is ultimately the cosmic Christ unfolding and fulfilling Himself.

In the evolutionary literature, Teilhard's position of objective idealism or spiritual monism had been held by Peirce and Royce. Vitalism had been advocated by Lamarck and Bergson. His concern for evolutionary creativity had been shared and expressed in the systems of Alexander, Sellars, Smuts, and Morgan. However, others differed from Teilhard. In the Kantian tradition, Spencer and Fiske acknowledged that ultimate reality is unknowable. (In his later works, Fiske's Christian orientation modified his original position to a religious interpretation.) But in sharp contrast to the Jesuit-priest's ontological commitment, Nietzsche, Haeckel, Marx, Engels, and Lenin held naturalistic positions. (For sure,

---

[21]*Ibid.*, p. 98.
[22]*Ibid.*, p. 119.
[23]*Ibid.*, p. 149.

Teilhard has been the only evolutionist to equate Christ with the cosmos.)

B. THE OBJECTIVE IDEALISM OF PEIRCE AND ROYCE

Since Charles Sanders Peirce (1839-1914) held that philosophy requires thorough-going evolutionism, his doctrine of pragmatism supported an evolutionary perspective. Writing at the close of the nineteenth century, he recognized three basic theories of evolution that were advocated in the literature: Darwinism, Cataclysmal, Lamarkian:

> Three modes of evolution have thus been brought before us; evolution by fortuitous variation, evolution by mechanical necessity, and evolution by creative love. We may term them *tychastic* evolution, or *tychasm, anacastic* evolution, or *anacasm,* and *agapastic* evolution, or *agapasm.* The doctrine which represent these as severally of principal importance we may term *tychasticism, anacasticism,* and *agapasticism.* On the other hand the mere propositions that absolute chance, mechanical necessity, and the law of love are severally operative in the cosmos may receive the names of *tychism, anacism,* and *agapism.*[24]

For Peirce, evolution is the cosmic growth of concrete reasonableness in which all three modes of the evolution of organic species cited have been operative. But like Teilhard, he favored the *agapastic* interpretation of evolution and asserted that the universe is a living organism. To account for the *origin* of the universe (a crucial point which Teilhard neglected to discuss),[25] he held that there had been:

> . . . . a state of just nothing at all, not even a state of emptiness, for even emptiness is something . . . an initial condition in which

---

[24]Charles Sanders Peirce: Evolutionary Love. *The Monist, 3*:188; 1893.

[25]Teilhard favored the "big-bang" theory over the "steady-state" and "oscillating" theories of the cosmos, as it was more compatible with his own view of a spindle-shaped universe. It is certainly safe to assume that Teilhard held to a single Creation or cosmogenesis originating from God-Omega (which he likened to Lemaître's primitive atom) at the Alpha Point. See, Pierre Teilhard de Chardin: *Man's Place in Nature: The Human Zoological Group.* New York, Harper and Row, 1966, p. 116.

the whole universe was nonexistent, and therefore a state of absolute nothing.[26]

Peirce taught that from this state of pure zero or unbounded potentiality there originated by evolutionary logic, i.e. the logic of freedom or potentiality, a state of potential consciousness. The evolutionary actualization of this state of potentiality began from nothing but an undifferentiated continuum of pure feeling. From this primordial chaos of unpersonalized feeling and pure chance evolved arbitrary brute force or action, followed by living intelligence. Therefore, we have three different but successive modes of metaphysical Being: feeling, antirational action, and rational thought. In short, the cosmos continues to evolve from its past state of homogeneity, chaos, and absolute chance to a future state of heterogeneity, maximum beauty, and complete order or concrete reasonableness.

Like Teilhard, Peirce had conceived cosmic evolution as a general, continuous tendency or "synechism" of increasing habit and decreasing chance toward an inevitable, absolutely perfect, rational and symmetrical goal. And his objective idealism was explicit:

> . . . as for the cosmos, only so far as it yet is mind, and so has life, is it capable of further evolution . . . remembering that all matter is really mind.[27]

Like Peirce, Josiah Royce (1855-1916) was also greatly influenced by Charles Darwin's *The Origin of Species* (1859) and adopted an evolutionary perspective. He made the needed distinction between the empirical *doctrine* of evolution and a *philosophy* of evolution, i.e. we have the distinction between scientific evidence and philosophical concepts:

> A *doctrine* of evolution may be, like Darwin's doctrine of natural selection, a purely empirical theory, a generalization from facts with a use of the postulates of science, and nothing more. How nature came by this seemingly ideal character of her processes, such an empirical doctrine need not try to explain. But a *philosophy* of evolu-

---

[26]Charles Sanders Peirce: *Collected Papers.* Cambridge, Harvard University Press, 1931, vol. 6, p. 147.

[27]Peirce: Evolutionary Love, pp. 178, 187.

tion, if there is ever to be one, must face just that ultimate question, Has the world a meaning? and, as a philosopher of a true *evolution*, must answer that question in the affirmative; for a philosophy, or at all events an affirmative, a positive philosophy, is, as we have seen all along, an effort to express, and by criticism to establish, the presuppositions of the age which it reflects upon. Now the presumption of an historical age is that there is a history embodied in the known world, and a philosophy of evolution must be an effort to give voice to this presupposition. If there is anything true in a philosophy of evolution, then there is something *more* than mere physical causation, mere mechanism in the world; for how there can be history in the world, no causal explanation, no appeal to mechanism as such, can ever directly express.[28]

Both Royce and Teilhard held that Darwinism was not sufficient to account for the *meaning* of evolution. Like Teilhard, Royce advocated a spiritualistic interpretation:

Hence it is that I love to study science. And when I study science I do so naively, submissively, straightforwardly, just as if the atoms and the suns and the milky-ways, the brains and the nerve-cells and and the reflex mechanisms, were all things in themselves. They aren't things in themselves; they are mere manifestations of the Self. . . . The more one becomes absorbed in the study of the wonders of nature, the nearer must lie the thought, that these things are not what they seem; that space and time, matter and motion, and life and our human consciousness, are but the show, the finite embodiment, the temporal manifestation, of a deeper truth.[29]
. . . . at bottom, the contrast between Mind and Matter is not as ultimate as it seems. . . . What we call matter would be a mere external appearance of the very sort of fact that we ourselves better know as Mind.[30]

Teilhard and Royce are very similar, although Royce did not have the rigorous scientific foundation that gave Teilhard's writings an air of truth. For Royce, the whole universe is a collectivity of selves evolving at different time-rates. This collectivity of selves is held to be identical with an Absolute Individual. And

---

[28]Josiah Royce: *The Spirit of Modern Philosophy*. New York, Norton, 1967, pp. 289-290.
[29]*Ibid.*, pp. 306, 312-313.
[30]Josiah Royce: *The World and the Individual*. New York, Dover, 1959, pp. 207, 213.

evolution is held to be the Life of God purposefully evolving toward a final unity of Absolute Consciousness. (There are no unconscious or preconscious regions in the universe, *only* conscious regions within an Eternal Order.)

Thus Teilhard's evolutionary monism had been presented in the works of Peirce and Royce. All three were objective idealists as a result of giving a privileged position to the status of mind or consciousness or spirit in the world. To be sure, there is a need to distinguish between the established facts of the sciences and conceptual frameworks. But a philosophy of evolution must consider these facts if it is to be valid. And it is assumptive reasoning to assume that the history of the world must have a meaning independent from human knowers who construct systems and constitute meanings. In short, the overextension of the place of human experience in the historical scheme of things results in a false metaphysics, i.e. an unwarranted ontology and cosmology.

C. THE VITALISM OF LAMARCK AND BERGSON

Vitalism has been advocated by authors of biologically oriented systems of evolution, but is best represented in the words of Lamarck and Bergson.

Carolus Linnaeus was perhaps the greatest biologist since Aristotle.[31] He revived, greatly expanded, and systematized taxonomy

---

[31]Although assigning man a definite place in the order of primates, Linnaeus (1707-1778) gave a Christian interpretation of nature. In *Systema Naturae* (1735), he held that God's existence was demonstrated in: (a) the nonmaterial, immortal, rational souls of man; (b) the "progenitorial unity" of organic development, i.e. like begets like; (c) the adaptive harmony between animals and their environment established through adequate senses. Although the father of modern taxonomy, Linnaeus held that his classification system of binomial nomenclature supported Aristotle's nonevolutionary "Great Chain of Being." Ironically, his system of phylogenetic classification would constitute a major evidence for an evolutionary interpretation of nature, as it implied common ancestries for similar species. (For evolutionary thought in the French Enlightenment see, Julien Offray de La Mettrie's *Man a Machine* (1748), George Louis Leclerc, Count de Buffon's *Historie Naturelle* (1749), Paul Dietrich, Baron D'Holbach's *System of Nature* (1770), and Denis Diderot's *Thoughts on the Interpretation of Nature* (1754) and *Elements of Physiology* (1780). The concept of evolution was present, but empirical evidence was wanting.)

(and referred to man as *Homo sapiens*). Yet both Aristotle, the father of biology, and Linnaeus held to the fixity of species, and therefore presented nonevolutionary views of the universe.

It was Jean-Baptiste-Pierre-Antonine de Monet, Chevalier de Lamarck (1744-1829) who wrote the first significant and "comprehensive" philosophy of evolution. He held to transformationism or the mutability of species, while his philosophical contemporary, Georg Wilhelm Friedrich Hegel (1770-1831), did not. (Hegel had restricted himself to the development of States and consciousness, but his historical approach was an advancement over dogmatic fixity.) In *The Philosophy of Zoology* (1809), Lamarck argued for vitalism:

> We cannot conceive the production of this phenomenon, that is to say, the presence and continuance of the movements constituting active life, unless we imagine a special exciting cause of these movements, a force which animates the organs, controls the activities and all the organic functions,—a spring, in short, of which the permanent though variable tension is the driving energy of all vital movements.[32]

Lamarck held that there was a continuous, innate, perfecting tendency within organic evolution as the result of the actions of vitalistic energies. He had postulated that such energies (or special, invisible vital fluids) were maintained by sunlight, pervasive in Nature, and necessary for organic movement, change, and life. Evolution was the direct result of the actions of these vital fluids which were responsible for increasing the complexity of organization as well as the number of organs and faculties in biological organisms. (Likewise, Teilhard had maintained that *radial* energy was directly responsible for the increased complexity of interior arrangement and the degree of consciousness manifested as the result of this complexity in evolutionary products.)

Lamarck is primarily remembered for his doctrines of "Use and Disuse" and "The Inheritance of Acquired Characteristics" which he held were sufficient to account for the adaptive harmony

---

[32]J. B. Lamarck: *Zoological Philosophy*. New York, Hafner, 1963, p. 211. (Also see pp. 2, 47-48, 186, 188, 201-218, 243, 251, and 345 for references to vitalism.)

between organisms and their environment.[33] He taught that environmental changes and/or the actions of will, desires, needs, or habits of an organism could stimulate the innate special, invisible fluids to affect visible vital fluids which, in turn, make the necessary modifications in the proper organs and therefore allowing for the animal's survival.

Lamarck's vitalistic position was teleological, for he saw evolution as a continuous, single, linear succession of natural objects. They naturally arrange themselves in a hierarchy from the simplest and imperfect to the most complex and perfect, i.e. there is manifested in evolution a linear succession *by degree* from the protozoans to Man (recall the positions of Aristotle and Linnaeus).

Like Teilhard, Lamarck's position is anthropocentric. He saw species of plants and animals as degenerative forms, increasing in imperfection as they fall further away from man's apical position in the "Great Chain of Being." But unlike Teilhard's comprehensive study, Lamarck concentrated only on biological evolution and never held that the plant and animal kingdoms had had a common origin, i.e. that life was the evolutionary extension of prelife. (He held the mineral, plant, and animal kingdoms to be separate but manifesting evolution.)

Henri Bergson (1859-1941) is the most significant philosopher of evolution before Teilhard. He was knowledgeable of the sciences, particularly biology and psychology, and demonstrated a rigorous philosophical mind.

In reaction to the materialistic and mechanistic views of the last century, Bergson adopted an antirational methodology and a vitalistic as well as dualistic interpretation of evolution. His major work, *Creative Evolution* (1907), was widely read and had a profound influence upon the formulation of Teilhard's thought, jarring it from its Medieval indoctrination with its static orientation. It presented a comprehensive and systematic account of evolution, emphasizing its creativity and divergency.

Bergson's metaphysics of evolution rested upon the applica-

---

[33]For the formulation of Lamarck's two Laws of biological evolution see *Ibid.,* pp. 113, 115, and 119.

tion of intuition or "intellectual sympathy."[34] As a result, he unfortunately distinguished between space and time, as well as matter and life or mind. (At this same time Einstein was advocating a space-time continuum and the interchangeability of matter and energy.) He held that only by the application of intuition could one hope to grasp an awareness of ultimate reality, which he maintained was time or pure duration. He taught that the use of reason, i.e. the application of mathematics and logic, is limited for it merely *spatializes* the world and therefore distorts the flux of evolution. In short, he claimed that the intellect gives us science which is relative knowledge of phenomena, while intuition is capable of giving us metaphysics which is absolute knowledge of reality. From these two opposing methodologies, Bergson assumed two ontological aspects of reality: matter and consciousness. (Now Teilhard saw the evolution of the stuff of the universe, i.e. *radial* energy, within a space-time continuum. And although he did rely upon intuition and mysticism to supplement rational knowledge, he never held the intellect to be falsifying in nature as Bergson maintained.)

Bergson taught that intuition not only discloses the flux of personality (the *durée reelle*) when applied subjectively, but also reveals the continuous fluidity of the evolution of nature (the *élan vital*) when applied objectively. He resorted to a metaphysical principle, the *élan vital* or spiritual force, in order to sufficiently account for the fluidity, continuity, irreversibility, creativity, and divergency manifested in an accumulative evolution which increases the complexity and consciousness of biological organisms. In short, his vitalistic position had been a philosophical compromise between mechanism and finalism, although he leaned toward the latter position:

> It is of no use to hold up before our eyes the dazzling prospect of a universal mathematic; we cannot sacrifice experience to the requirements of a system. That is why we reject radical mechanism. But radical finalism is quite as unacceptable, and for the same reason. . . . Finalism thus understood is only inverted mechanism. . . .

[34]For a brief introduction and explanation of Bergson's intuitive methodology see Henri Bergson: *An Introduction to Metaphysics.* New York, Bobbs-Merrill, 1955.

The error of radical finalism, as also that of radical mechanism, is to extend too far the application of certain concepts that are natural to our intellect. . . . Both doctrines are reluctant to see in the course of things generally, or even simply in the development of life, an unforeseeable creation of form.[35]

(Descartes, Spinoza, and Leibniz had attempted to represent reality through mathematical methodologies. And Husserl spoke of a "geometry" of experience, a *mathesis universalis*.)

In order to account for the creativity or novelty in evolution, Bergson had postulated a vital impetus that runs through the otherwise static matter of the world. He was aware that such a metaphysical principle was unverifiable, but nevertheless it conceptually accounted for the emergence of new, unpredictable forms:[36]

. . . the "vital principle" may indeed not explain much, but it is at least a sort of label affixed to our ignorance, so as to remind us of this occasionally, while mechanism invites us to ignore that ignorance.[37]

Like Teilhard, Bergson saw evolution as the growth of complexity and consciousness, although he taught that matter and mind represented different ontological realms. Creative evolution *externally* diverged into the plant, insect, and animal kingdoms, while *internally* it manifested the emergence of vegetative torpor, instinct, and intelligence (as well as intuition and mysticism) respectively. And although he distinguished between the within and without of things, there was no Teilhardian "reduction" to a psychic monism. He maintained a dualism, but did give a privileged position to mind:

The evolution of life, looked at from this point, receives a clearer meaning. . . . It is as if a broad current of consciousness had penetrated matter, loaded, as all consciousness is, with an enormous mul-

---

[35]Henri Bergson: *Creative Evolution*. New York, The Modern Library, 1944, pp. 45, 50, 51.

[36]The philosophers of evolution have emphasized the emergence of creativity or novelty, often resorting to metaphysical forces or entities as an ultimate explanation. Yet all of them, including Teilhard, unfortunately lacked a sufficient understanding of genetics.

[37]*Ibid.*, pp. 48-49.

tiplicity of interwoven potentialities. It has carried matter along to organization, but its movement has been at once infinitely retarded and infinitely divided. . . . If our analysis is correct, it is consciousness, or rather supra-consciousness, that is at the origin of life. . . . Finally, consciousness is essentially free; it is freedom itself; but it cannot pass through matter without settling on it, without adapting itself to it. . . . Matter or mind, reality has appeared to us as a perpetual becoming.[38]

(It is worth noting here that Teilhard too had maintained that ultimately consciousness or *radial* energy is free.) [39]

There are great similarities and differences between Teilhard and Bergson. In general, Bergson's system is dualistic, vitalistic, and open. Teilhard's system is monistic, teleological, and closed. Both held evolution to be a creative, irreversible, irreducible, and vitalistic process. And both emphasized the increasing complexity, consciousness, and mysticism unfolding within it.

In short, where Bergson saw planetary evolution as a *diverging* process within a quasi-pantheistic orientation, Teilhard held that it was a *converging* process capable of supporting a theistic orientation. Their major differences are due to methodological procedure and personal motives. Despite their shortcomings from a naturalistic approach, the author believes that Bergson and Teilhard represent the two most significant philosophies of evolution in this century because of their sincere concern for time and human survival respectively.

Vitalism is a metaphysical doctrine advocating a Life-giving entity or substance independent of matter. From Aristotle to Driesch, forms of vitalism have been given to account for biological phenomena. But modern evolutionary biology renders them pseudoexplanations. Life is an emergent property due to new organizations and relations of matter and energy. As such, it is subject to further empirical investigation.

D. THE EMERGENT EVOLUTIONISTS

Unlike the naive vitalists who abstracted Life from matter and then gave it ontological autonomy, the emergent evolutionists

---

[38]*Ibid.*, pp. 199, 284, 294, 296.
[39]*The Phenomenon of Man*, pp. 57, 110-111, 149, 307-308.

took a naturalistic orientation and held organic phenomena to be the continuation of inorganic phenomena. The evolution of the stuff of the universe accounted for the emergence of new properties, including life. The systems of Alexander, Sellars, Smuts, and Morgan represent the most important work done in emergent evolution. Although they differ considerably, they all shared Teilhard's interest in evolutionary creativity and novelty without resorting to objective idealism.

In his major work, *Space, Time, and Deity* (1920), Samuel Alexander (1859-1938) gave a metaphysical analysis of the emergence of qualities within a space-time continuum. He distinguished between Space-Time or Motion as an objective, continuous, infinite whole, and the finite, homogeneous units of space-time or motion that fill this infinity. That is, the stuff or substance of the infinite universe is Space-Time or Motion of which finite space-times or motions are merely fragments. (He also referred to these cosmic units as point-instants or finite extensions, durations, or pure events. Unlike Teilhard, they are not homogeneous units of psychic energy; and Teilhard never taught that the universe was infinite.)

Alexander taught that within this *plenum* there is a nisus or creative tendency. As a result of this innate tendency, Space-Time or Motion generates a chronological hierarchy of new, finite, "empirical" qualities. The successive order of emergent qualities is held to be as follows:

D_1 motions
D_2 materiality with primary, constant qualities
D_3 materiality with secondary, variable qualities
D_4 life (organic)
D_5 mind (consciousness)
D_6 deity[40]

Like Alexander, Teilhard distinguished between cosmic units, matter or pre-life, life, mind or consciousness, and God. But it should be noted that for Alexander each new emergent quality is the deity in respect to the previous emergent quality. This differs

---

[40]Samuel Alexander: *Space, Time, and Deity*. New York, Dover, 1966, vol. 2, pp. 45-73.

significantly from Teilhard's theistic orientation, and we shall refer to this difference when we consider Teilhard's formulation of an Omega Point.

Alexander's metaphysical scheme holds that matter is derived from units of space-time or motion. In light of our present understanding of the physical world, this aspect adds nothing to a science-oriented philosophy.

Roy Wood Sellars (b. 1880) adopted a   position of critical realism or evolutionary naturalism. His doctrine of emergent evolution was a reaction against Platonism and Kantianism. Epistemologically, it advocated a position of critical and physical realism. Metaphysically, it held to emergent materialism.

Sellars took time, evolution, creative synthesis, novelty, and accumulative growth seriously, and held there was a discoverable orderliness, massiveness, and immanent executiveness about nature. Nature represented a four-dimensional manifold of space-time, and manifested the four primary categories of space, time, thinghood, and causality. Evolution implies novelty and genetic continuity, and has resulted in distinct levels of development but not levels of reality. That is, matter is active and capable of high levels of organization and accumulation, resulting in the emergence of new properties by *degree:*

> Evolution seems to mean that the higher is built on the lower or is an integration of the lower. . . . I mean that the higher order implies and includes the lower order. . . . The ladder of evolved forms teaches the lesson that novelty may be added to novelty to produce novelties of higher orders. . . . And yet this rise of higher levels must rest upon and but carry out the potentialities of the lower levels.[41]

Sellars held that the logical structure of nature or emergent evolution revealed a hierarchy of a pyramid or tier-like construction representing stages or levels of complexity of organization and *degrees of freedom,* as well as new laws and categories. Historically, the general levels are represented by matter, life, mind, and society:

---

[41]Roy Wood Sellars: *Evolutionary Naturalism*. Chicago, The Open Court Publishing Company, 1922, pp. 160, 261, 335.

Matter, itself, was evolved. Then came the earth with its waters, its salts, and fertile earth and, giving it radiant energy, the sun. Then little by little came life reaching upward to more complex forms. . . . Slowly life lifted to mind, the human mind being the latest and highest to appear. Pre-history gave way to human history and society with its fruit, civilization, began to dominate the surface of the earth.[42]

Although like Teilhard in viewing the structure of evolution as a pyramid, Sellars does not imply teleology, i.e. nature is not evolving according to a predetermined design and end:

We must rid the term of any finalism and be ready to admit that any change is the function of conditions. . . . There seems no reason to continue this anthropomorphism which makes events a mere rehearsal of an established plan.[43]

Sellars' nonreductive materialistic ontology and evolutionary cosmology are in line with the advancement of the special sciences (and his humanism and democratic socialism are in the best interests of the human condition) .

Jan Christian Smuts' (1870-1950) philosophy of Holism was an attempt to reconcile the conflicting views and implications of mechanism and vitalism. In *Holism and Evolution* (1925), he presented a holistic and creative interpretation of planetary evolution within a non-Euclidean universe, i.e. within a curved or warped space-time continuum. Within the creative synthesis of evolution, he taught that Matter, Life, Mind, and Personality represented the successive major advances of cosmic energy. He held that the universe is ultimately intensely active Energy or Action. Matter is concentrated structural energy or action that is active, plastic, and transmutable, i.e. capable of manifesting creative forms or arrangements or patterns and values.

Smuts taught that the fundamental factor of the universe is its *wholeness*. Wholeness is the basic characteristic and tendency of events within the geometrical progression of cosmic development from necessity to greater degrees of freedom. In short, holism

---

[42]Roy Wood Sellars: *The Principles and Problems of Philosophy*. New York, Macmillan, 1926, p. 363.

[43]Sellars: *Evolutionary Naturalism*, pp. 261, 272.

is the ultimate category from which are derived the physical, chemical, organic, psychical, and personal categories of nature:

> Evolution is nothing but the gradual development and stratification of progressive series of wholes, stretching from the inorganic beginnings to the highest levels of spiritual creation. . . . And the progressive development of the resulting wholes at all stages—from the most inchoate, imperfect, inorganic wholes to the most highly developed and organised, is what we call Evolution. . . . Thus there arises a progressive scale of wholes, rising from the material bodies of inorganic nature through the plant and animal kingdoms to man and the great ideal and artistic creations of the spiritual world. . . . From the more or less homogeneous to the heterogeneous; from heterogeneous multiplicity again to greater, more advanced harmony, to a harmonious co-operative ordered unity; such a formula may serve as a rough-and-ready description of the holistic process.[44]

Unlike Teilhard, Smuts' view of evolution is naturalistic with no resort to spiritualism, teleology, or an Absolute. Although his holistic factor remains inscrutable, he has given us a naturalistic framework.

In *Emergent Evolution* (1927) and *The Emergence of Novelty* (1933), C. Lloyd Morgan (1852-1936) presented a metaphysical scheme in which he discussed the emergence of new *kinds* of *intrinsic relatedness* among pre-existent, spatio-temporal events. He distinguished between three kinds of relatedness or natural systems: Matter, Life, and Mind, i.e. physico-chemical, vital, and conscious events. Matter, Life, and Mind represent distinct emergent levels within which there are qualitative differences.

For Morgan, evolution is a progressive advance with novelty, or the actualization of enfolded possibilities:

> According to emergent evolution, as I seek to develop its thesis, there is an ascending hierarchy of kinds or orders of relatedness ranging from those that obtain in the atom, in the molecule, in the crystal, and so on near the base of the pyramid, to that of an order of reflective consciousness near the apex.[45]

---

[44]Jan Christian Smuts: *Holism and Evolution.* New York, Viking Press, 1961, pp. v, 99, 105, 232.

[45]C. Lloyd Morgan: *Emergent Evolution.* New York, Henry Holt and Company, 1927, p. 148.

Like Teilhard, the emergent evolutionists had reacted against mechanistic interpretations of evolution. They held that such interpretations fail to sufficiently account for the creative or novel advance of evolution. Unlike Teilhard, they did not resort to objective idealism. Alexander, Sellars, Smuts, and Morgan had seen emergent evolution ontologically grounded in matter or energy or motion. But Alexander, Sellars, and Morgan had anticipated Teilhard's thought when they represented the structure of emergent evolution as a pyramid. Only Morgan resorted to the influence of God to account for the creative advance of the evolutionary process. (We shall refer to his similarity to Teilhard's thought when we consider the Omega Point.)

E. THE COSMIC VIEWS OF SPENCER AND FISKE

Herbert Spencer (1820-1903) and John Fiske (1842-1901) presented the first truly cosmic philosophies of evolution. From their cosmic orientation, they held that all forms of phenomena are interrelated through evolution. But in the Kantian tradition, they distinguished between the Knowable and the Unknowable, i.e. between appearance and reality. Like Teilhard, they attempted to reconcile science and religion by showing the limitations of empirical inquiry.

Spencer's evolutionary cosmology is presented in his *First Principles* (1862), the first volume of his "Synthetic Philosophy." He had conceived the doctrine of evolution as a universal process embracing all the manifestations of the cosmos. And he held that there must be an *a priori* Law governing the phenomena of astronomy, geology, biology, sociology, psychology, and ethics.

Lamarck's Laws of evolution had been restricted to the animal kingdom, for he had held that the mineral, vegetable, and animal worlds were independent in their origin. But Spencer's cosmic Law allowed for no such breaks as it presented the universe as a continuous process.[46] His "Synthetic Philosophy" rested upon three major assumptions:

---

[46]Like Spencer, Teilhard desired to establish an all-embracing Law of evolution. He held that such a cosmic Law would demonstrate purpose and direction in the development of the universe. Likewise, he will argue that a cosmic design infers a Designer, i.e. a Supreme Mind.

1. The cosmos is divided into a Knowable realm and an Unknowable realm.
2. Matter, Motion, Space, and Time are manifestations of Force. This is his doctrine of "The Persistence of Force."
3. The cosmos passes through an infinite series of finite and unique cycles. Each cycle manifests three successive stages of Evolution, Equilibration, and Dissolution.

Unlike Teilhard, Spencer held that theism, as well as atheism and pantheism, was "absolutely unthinkable." Yet he maintained that science and religion are necessarily correlatives but limited in their ability to discern the ultimate nature of the universe. For Spencer, they were reconciled in the fact that the Power of the universe is utterly inscrutable.

Both Spencer and Fiske had as a common denominator the beilef in an Unknowable realm, i.e. the Unconditioned or ultimate reality existing behind the appearances of the cosmos. (We recall Kant's distinction between the noumena and the phenomena.) Spencer, in short, held that the ontology of the universe is absolutely incomprehensible to the human understanding and therefore forever unknowable. And as a result, all knowledge is only relative and can never be absolute.

Yet Spencer held that Force is the "ultimate of ultimates." Space, Time, Matter, and Motion are merely conscious abstractions from the experiences of persisting Force which, in turn, is immediately produced from an Absolute Reality. Force is the bridge between the Knowable and the Unknowable:

> Force, as we know it, can be regarded only as a certain conditioned effect of the Unconditioned Cause—as the relative reality indicating to us an Absolute Reality by which it is immediately produced. . . .
> The sole truth which transcends experience by underlying it, is thus the Persistence of Force.[47]

To account for all the phenomena in the universe as it progressed as a single metamorphosis as well as to express simultaneously the complex antecedents and the complex consequences

---

[47]Herbert Spencer: *First Principles.* New York, The De Witt Revolving Fund, Inc., 1958, pp. 175, 200. For references on the Unknowable see, pp. 60, 79, 80, 93, 118, 119, 120, 163, 166, 174, 191-192, 199, 281.

of such phenomena, Spencer formulated an *a priori* cosmic Law. He held that it both inductively and deductively satisfied the evolutionary unity of all concrete phenomena. His final formulation of the cosmic Law of Evolution was as follows:

> Evolution is an integration of matter and concomitant dissipation of motion; during which the matter passes from an indefinite, incoherent homogeneity to a definite, coherent heterogeneity; and during which the retained motion undergoes a parallel transformation.[48]

Spencer held that the cosmic process of evolution, both in its simple and compound manifestations, advances in a geometrical progession. We have the accelerating increase of heterogeneity toward a stage of cosmic equilibration and quiescence in which the most extreme multiformity and most complex moving equilibrium are established. The duration of this stage is limited, for he held that it was followed by universal Dissolution, an inevitable complement or counter movement of universal Evolution. As a result, Spencer gives us a cosmology necessarily cyclical. As a result, his "Theory of Things" presents an eternal alteration of Evolution and Dissolution in the "totality of things." (We shall see that Spencer's cyclical cosmology differs from Friedrich Nietzsche's Doctrine of Eternal Recurrence and Teilhard's conception of a single, converging cycle.)

Spencer's evolutionary cycles are successive, infinite in number, and analogous in principles but *not identical:*

> Apparently, the universally-coexistent forces of attraction and repulsion, which, as we have seen, necessitate rhythm in all minor changes throughout the Universe, also necessitate rhythm in the totality of its changes—produce now an immeasurable period during which the attractive forces predominating, cause universal concentration, and then an immeasureable period during which the repulsive forces predominating, cause universal diffusion—alternate eras of Evolution and Dissolution. And thus there is suggested the conception of a past during which there have been successive Evolutions analogous to that which is now going on; and a future during which successive other such Evolutions may go on—ever the same in principle but never the same in concrete result.[49]

---

[48]*Ibid.,* p. 394.
[49]*Ibid.,* p. 529.

For if, as we saw reason to think, there is an alternation of Evolution and Dissolution in the totality of things—if, as we are obliged to infer from the Persistence of Force, the arrival at either limit of this vast rhythm brings about the conditions under which a countermovement commences—if we are hence compelled to entertain the conception of Evolutions that have filled an immeasurable past and Evolutions that will fill an immeasurable future; we can no longer contemplate the visible creation as having a definite beginning or end, or as being isolated. It becomes unified with all existence before and after; and the Force which the Universe presents, falls into the same category with its Space and Time, as admitting of no limitation in thought.[50]

(We shall see that Nietzsche held to an infinite number of successive, finite cosmic cycles of evolution and dissolution, each, however, being *absolutely identical*.)

Although Spencer held that the Force which connected the conditioned Phenomenal order with the unconditioned Noumenal order to be forever inscrutable, he taught that it was persistent and eternal. He was a naturalist, and as such never suggested that such a Force was psychic in nature.

Like Teilhard, Spencer's sociology viewed society as a superorganism. Like a biological organism, he taught that society increases in mass, complexity, integration or interdependence, and formally endures independent of its units which are born, develop, and die. He held that social evolution ended in equilibrium, while Teilhard taught that psycho-social evolution had a divine destination.

Fiske's *Outlines of Cosmic Philosophy, Based on the Doctrine of Evolution, with Criticism on the Positive Philosophy* (1874) was a reinstatement, with additions, of Spencer's "Synthetic Philosophy."[51] His own major contribution to evolutionary theory was his doctrine of the significance of the prolongation of the period of infancy as a factor in the evolution of mankind. He taught that the need for the prolonged care and education of hu-

---

[50]*Ibid.*, p. 542.

[51]For his own additions to Spencer's work see, John Fiske: *Outlines of Cosmic Philosophy, Based on the Doctrine of Evolution, with Criticisms on the Positive Philosophy*. New York, Houghton, Mifflin and Company, 1902, part II, vols. 3 and 4, chap. 18-22.

man infants explained the origin of the family, made the accumulation of knowledge and therefore the improvement of society possible, and contributed to the growth of altruism.[52]

Fiske was concerned with the relation of philosophy to religion, and, like Kant and Spencer, originally held that there is an independent reality beyond consciousness which is essentially Unknowable (Kant held that the three metaphysical questions of God, immortality, and free will belonged to the Noumenal or Unknowable realm but were necessary for the operation of the rational Categorical Imperative; in short, the alleged limitations of science gave way for a moral argument for God, immortality, and free will). His final thought replaced Spencer's mechanical view with a theistic and teleological interpretation of the process of evolution:

> The advance of modern science carries us irresistibly to what some German philosophers call monism, but I prefer to call it monotheism. In getting rid of the Devil and regarding the universe as the multiform manifestation of a single all-pervading Deity, we become for the first time pure and uncompromising monotheists,—believers in the ever-living, unchangeable, and all-wise Heavenly Father, in whom we may declare our trust without the faintest trace of mental reservation.[53]

Both Spencer and Fiske have presented highly assumptive cosmologies. It is unwarranted to overextend a biological model to account for the process of the whole knowable cosmos. Different phenomena, although a part of the same universe, require their own peculiar methods and principles. And it is dogmatic to place closure on human inquiry by maintaining an *a priori* Unknowable realm. The distinction between the Known and Unknown is sufficient. However, their cosmic orientation is desirable as it prevents the formulation of a myopic perspective.

---

[52]See Philip P. Wiener: *Evolution and the Founders of Pragmatism.* New York, Harper and Row, 1965, pp. 129-151.

[53]John Fiske: *Through Nature to God.* New York, Houghton, Mifflin, 1899, p. 22.

F. THE EVOLUTIONARY NATURALISTS

In Germany, Friedrich Nietzsche (1844-1900) and Ernst Haeckel (1834-1919) had adopted materialistic interpretations of evolution. The motion of matter, not the development of mind, constituted the basis of the universe. There was no need to resort to religious assumptions to account for man's proper place in the cosmos. Religion is a human construction to be replaced by the advancement of scientific understanding.

Nietzsche's cosmology was derived from his central doctrine of Eternal Recurrence, which he referred to as his "great cultivating and triumphant idea."[54] He had rejected Platonism, Kantianism, Christianity, pantheism, and teleology in favor of a naturalistic interpretation of cosmic evolution. His doctrine was grounded in the law of the conservation of matter and energy, the eternality of time, and the finitude of space. He argued that if the world manifests a finite quantity of force, i.e. matter or energy, then cosmic evolution could only manifest a certain definite number of possible combinations or events. Therefore, the entire evolutionary sequence would eventually duplicate itself in the same manner. As a result, Nietzsche held that there was an eternal series of finite, absolutely identical, cyclical evolutions:

> The eternal hourglass of existence is turned over and over, and you with it, a dust grain of dust. . . . Everything goes, everything comes back; eternally rolls the wheel of being. Everything dies, everything blossoms again; eternally runs the year of being. Everything breaks, everything is joined anew; eternally the same house of being is built. Everything parts, everything greets every other thing again; eternally the ring of being remains faithful to itself. . . . Bent is the path of eternity. . . . We have already existed an eternal number of times, and all things with us.[55]

> To the paralyzing sense of general disintegration and incompleteness I oppose the *eternal recurrence*. . . . In place of "metaphysics"

---

[54]Nietzsche formulated his concept of Eternal Recurrence in 1881, the year of Teilhard's birth.

[55]Friedrich Nietzsche: *The Portable Nietzsche*. New York, Viking Press, 1968, pp. 101, 329, 332. Also see, pp. 98, 101-102, 257, 269-270, 327-333, 339-340, 364, 430, 434, 435, 436, 459, 563.

and religion, the theory of recurrence. . . . That *everything recurs is the closest approximation of a world of becoming to a world of being.* . . . An anti-metaphysical view of the world—yes, but an artistic one.[56]

Nietzsche referred to his doctrine as a *"circulus vitiosus deus."* It is significant for us because it represents a break from German idealism in favor of naturalism, i.e. a materialistic ontology. Like Nietzsche, Haeckel also adopted a naturalistic orientation and attacked the Church for its spiritualistic orientation.

Haeckel devoted his life to defending Darwin's theory of biological evolution. But he also considered the philosophical implications of cosmic evolution on the nature of man and his proper place in the universe. In his major philosophical work, *The Riddle of the Universe at the Close of the Nineteenth Century* (1900), Haeckel argued for a "Monistic Philosophy," defending materialism and pantheism. He rejected the three dogmas of "anthropism" which he held misrepresented the true nature of man:

1. The *anthropocentric* dogma, which maintains that man is the pre-ordained centre and aim of all terrestrial life. Here Haeckel differs from Teilhard's teleology, in which human evolution is seen as the continuation of biological evolution and goal-directed.

2. The *anthropomorphic* dogma, which maintains that God, the creator, sustainer, and ruler of the world, has human attributes, and as a result man is god-like. He rejects all forms of theism, but adopts a pantheistic position. Teilhard held that a Personal Centre was necessary to explain the origin, sustainment, and goal of evolution. He held that belief in the existence of God was necessary for human survival and adopted a position of evolutionary panentheism.

3. The *anthropolatric* dogma, which maintains ontological dualism and the personal immortality of the human soul. Haeckel adopted a pervasive materialism while Teilhard taught pervasive spiritualism and argued for the immortality of the human soul.[57]

---

[56]Friedrich Nietzsche: *The Will to Power.* New York, Vintage Books, 1968, pp. 224, 255, 330, 539. Also see pp. 35-39, 340, 344. Nietzsche was planning to write a book, *The Eternal Recurrence.* For his last remarks concerning his doctrine, see pp. 544-550. When Nietzsche refers to the Eternal Recurrence as being an anti-metaphysical doctrine he means anti-theological, for his concept is not scientifically verifiable and therefore remains assumptive.

[57]Ernst Haeckel: *The Riddle of the Universe at the Close of the Nineteenth Century.* New York, Harper and Brothers, 1900, pp. 11-13. For a summary of Haeckel's position see pp. 13-14.

Haeckel held that the "riddle of the universe" was to discern its ontological status. He taught that the "Law of Substance," as a result of the eternal persistence of matter and force, called for a naturalistic interpretation. It was grounded in two great scientific theorems:

1. The Conservation of Matter. Lavoisier's chemical law of the persistence or indestructibility of matter (1789).
2. The Conservation of Energy. Mayer and Helmholtz's physical law of the persistence or indestructibility of force (1842).

For Haeckel, the two cosmic laws were fundamentally one. Their unity was expressed as the "law of the persistence of matter and force." He referred to it as the fundamental cosmic "Law of Substance" which supported universal unity, continuity, and causality, while ruling out the three central dogmas of Christian metaphysics:[58]

> Our monistic view, that the great cosmic law applies throughout the whole of nature, is of the highest moment. For it not only involves, on its positive side, the essential unity of the cosmos and the causal connection of all phenomena that come within our cognizance, but it also, in a negative way, marks the highest intellectual progress, in that it definitely rules out the three central dogmas of metaphysics—God, freedom, and immortality. In assigning mechanical causes to phenomena everywhere, the law of substance comes into line with the universal law of causality.[59]

Haeckel's naturalistic monism is in direct opposition to Teilhard's spiritualistic monism. And Teilhard held to the three dogmas of "anthropism." But Nietzsche and Haeckel were not alone in maintaining materialism. Marx, Engels, and Lenin had been influenced by the evolutionary theory and held naturalistic interpretations.

Karl Marx's (1818-1883) natural attitude was in direct opposition to Hegel's phenomenological attitude which had ignored man as a historico-social being by grounding itself in a spiritualis-

---

[58]Haeckel's "Law of Substance" has benefitted by the implications of Einstein's theory of relativity. The interchangeability of matter and energy scientifically justifies a naturalistic monism. For matter and energy are merely two manifestations of the ontological unity of the universe. Teilhard had favored energy over matter, and then claimed that all energy was psychic in nature.

[59]*Ibid.*, p. 232.

tic monism. Marx, as well as Engels and Lenin, was a dialectical and historical materialist. He gave primacy to matter, and saw the universe as matter in dialectical development. Consciousness or mind was merely a natural activity, incapable of existing independent of man:

> . . . only naturalism is able to comprehend the process of world history. *Man* is directly a *natural being*. . . . Consciousness can never be anything else than conscious existence, and the existence of men is their actual life-process. . . . Life is not determined by consciousness, but consciousness by life. . . . Consciousness is therefore from the very beginning a social product, and remains so as long as men exist at all.[60]

And Engels (1820-1895) wrote:

> Modern natural science has had to take over from philosophy the principle of the indestructibility of motion; it cannot any longer exist without this principle. But the motion of matter is not merely crude mechanical motion, mere change of place, it is heat and light, electric and magnetic stress, chemical combination and dissociation, life and, finally, consciousness. . . . It is the nature of matter to advance to the evolution of thinking beings.[61]

V. I. Lenin (1870-1924) presents a naturalistic position in his *Materialism and Empirio-Criticism* (1909). He reacts against idealism and dualism by holding that the material world is independent of human cognition, man is a product of biological evolution, and "mind" is dependent upon matter, i.e. matter is prior to "mind:"

> Materialism is the recognition of "objects in themselves," or outside the mind; ideas and sensations are copies or images of those objects. . . . Materialism, in full agreement with natural science, takes matter primary and regards consciousness, thought and sensation as secondary, because in its well-defined form sensation is associated only with the higher forms of matter (organic matter), while "in the

---

[60]Erich Fromm: *Marx's Concept of Man.* New York, Ungar, 1967, pp. 181, 197, 198, 203.

[61]Frederick Engels: *Dialetics of Nature.* New York, International Publishers, 1963, pp. 21, 228. For a materialistic as well as Lamarckian interpretation of the bio-social transition from ape to man, see pp. 279-296. For a further discussion of Darwinism, see Frederick Engels: *Anti-Duhring.* New York, International, 1966, pp. 75-85.

foundation of the structure of matter" one can only surmise the existence of a faculty akin to sensation. . . . Matter is that which, acting upon our sense-organs, produces sensation; matter is the objective reality given to us in sensation, and so forth.[62]

It is the evolutionary perspective that allows Lenin to hold that inorganic matter is prior to organic matter, and organic matter prior to consciousness:

> No man in the least educated or in the least healthy doubts that the earth existed at a time when there *could not* have been any life on it. . . . Natural science positively asserts that the earth once existed in such a state that no man or any other creature existed or could have existed on it. Organic matter is a late phenomenon, the fruit of a long evolution. It follows that there was no sentient matter, no "complexes of sensations," no *self* that was supposedly "indissolubly" connected with the environment in accordance with Avenarius' doctrine. Matter is primary, and thought, consciousness, sensation are products of a very high development. Such is the materialist theory of knowledge, to which natural science instinctively prescribes.[63]

G. FINAL INTERPRETATION

Teilhard held that the universe has an *internal* structure not accessible to objective investigation. Therefore, it is necessary but not sufficient to deal with the external structure and complexity of things. He taught that the *internal* realm was more significant than the *external,* as its consideration provided the means for understanding the purpose and goal of planetary evolution.

The emergent evolutionists had seen consciousness only as a recent emergent property or quality. They had not, as Teilhard had done, traced its origins *as consciousness* back to the commencement of cosmic evolution.

Teilhard held that *all* the objects of nature have an *interior* as well as an *exterior.* Bergson had acknowledged this when he postulated that a stream of consciousness runs through the matter of the universe, and therefore formulated an unwarranted dualism. Teilhard rightly criticized the naturalists for ignoring the histori-

---

[62]V. I. Lenin: *Materialism and Empirio-Criticism: Critical Comments on a Reactionary Philosophy.* New York, International, 1927, pp. 17, 38, 145.
[63]*Ibid.,* pp. 72, 69.

cal development of consciousness in their mechanical and mechanistic conceptions of evolution. Even Nietzsche had expressed a desire to deal with the subjective field of inquiry:

> I maintain the phenomenality of the inner world, too. . . . I should like to form an image of the inner world, too, by means of some schema, and thus triumph over intellectual confusion.[64]

Teilhard's phenomenology of evolution was to account for the development of matter and mind. But like Peirce and Royce he grounded it in objective idealism. To do justice to the evolving interiority of the universe, Teilhard did injustice to its material foundation.

As a Jesuit-priest and scientist, Teilhard had desired to reconcile theism with naturalism. As a Christian, he rejected atheism, agnosticism, and pantheism. Likewise, he rejected materialism, dualism, and pluralism in favor of a monistic metaphysics. And since eschatology was always foremost in his thought, there was no compromising as far as ontology was concerned. To allow for the future convergence of nature with God, his faith took preference over science. Unlike the orthodox conceptions of theism, Teilhard established a spiritualistic panentheism that was both vitalistic and teleological. But his position is contrary to scientific knowledge and human experience.

The distinction between the Phenomenal and Noumenal worlds is untenable, for it leads to an ontological dualism. One should look at the universe from the position of perspectivals, i.e. there are an infinite number of possible perspectives of the *material* cosmos, of which the human perspective represents only one.

Teilhard has erroneously overextended the ontological position and importance of consciousness or mental activity. His spiritualistic monism is a religious bias. For his beliefs in a personal God, immortality of the human soul, and freedom of the human will are merely the results of religious enculturation. The distinction between epistemology and ontology or metaphysics is crucial. The universe is seldom the way we desire it to be.

---

[64]Nietzsche: *The Will to Power*, pp. 263, 324. The phenomenology of Edmund Husserl ignored the evolutionary perspective.

For Teilhard the universe was not grounded in matter or energy. He held that from its beginning to its end, the cosmos was nothing more or less than the growth of consciousness. But the emergence of consciousness on the earth as a natural activity is a recent event. And we may assume that consciousness represents only one quality of an infinite number of qualities possible in an eternal and infinite universe. This I believe should be the position held by a truly *cosmic* perspective. It does not belittle the significance of consciousness, but acknowledges its relative importance. It is anthropocentric to hold consciousness to be of primary importance.

Finally, we should consider Teilhard's vitalism and atomism. Philosophical concepts should supplement scientific knowledge, making isolated facts intelligible. The position of vitalism as represented in the works of Lamarck, Bergson, and Teilhard, although an attempt to account for creative activity in evolution, is untenable if it leads to the ontologizing of the concept as a separate force or agent. Science should be sufficient to account for evolutionary creativity. Teilhard's atomism presents a monadic universe of psychic units. It would be more accurate for an evolutionist to view the universe as a series of events grounded in matter or energy. Crude atomism distorts the continuity and fluidity of the universe.

In the last analysis, Teilhard's evolutionary monism is the result of a basic religious motive and misrepresents the true nature of things. A rigorous science-oriented philosophy acknowledges the primacy of matter or energy, and sees the human mind as a natural activity and the product of biological evolution. Further questions concerning the nature and structures of matter should be left to be resolved by further scientific inquiry.

Chapter III

TEILHARD'S LAW OF
COMPLEXITY - CONSCIOUSNESS

As a scientist, Teilhard had devoted his life to descriptive geology and paleontology. He was an expert on Chinese geology and specialized in vertebrate paleontology, concentrating on mammalian evolution.[1] But his interests shifted to primate evolution in general, and human paleontology in particular. His works were both analytic and synthetic, for every fact was quickly incorporated into an evolutionary framework. He taught that philosophy and science supplemented each other, and never failed to extend the implications of his "vision" to the future evolution of the human species; although he had been permitted to publish his strictly scientific articles, he was repeatedly warned not to delve into philosophy or theology. Fortunately, his popularizations of the Sinanthropus[2] material brought him worldwide fame and academic recognition.[3]

Copernicus had held that the geocentric model of the universe could be replaced by the heliocentric theory. Galileo gave the latter hypothesis scientific grounding, while Giordano Bruno[4] argued for an eternal and infinite universe with its center everywhere or nowhere. As a result, man's habitat no longer occupied a central position in the cosmos, for the earth was merely one heavenly body among innumerable other stars and planets. And it was even possible that sentient beings existed in other solar systems. Man's special position in nature had taken a serious blow.

---

[1] Teilhard expressed the desire to study geochemistry.

[2] Considered a pithecanthropoid, i.e. a member of the *Homo erectus* stage or level of human evolution.

[3] See Teilhard's *Man's Place in Nature: The Human Zoological Group, The Appearance of Man,* and *The Vision of the Past.* In these works Teilhard indirectly refers to the theo-philosophical implications.

[4] See Antoinette Mann Paterson: *The Infinite Worlds of Giordano Bruno.* Springfield, Thomas, 1970.

The theory of biological evolution had been anticipated in pre-Socratic thought.[5] But Aristotelian biology, holding to the fixity of species, prevented the development of an evolutionary perspective. This anti-evolutionary orientation dominated scientific thought until the Renaissance. Since the Church could no longer restrict biological investigations, naturalists became aware of the fluidity of nature and the close resemblances between man and the great apes. The evolutionary theory found its first serious formulation in the bold works of Lamarck. Yet the theory remained, for the most part, merely a provisional, working hypothesis at best. It was not until Darwin's works, supported by empirical evidence, that man was squarely placed in the order of primates. Man was no longer a descended angel, as had been taught, but an ascended "ape." The author believes that the investigations and writings of Galileo and Darwin have contributed more to a scientific understanding of the proper place of man in the universe than the works of any other thinkers. They have successfully eliminated geocentrism and anthropocentrism from a scientific oriented cosmology. From this new perspective the writings of Teilhard represent a regression in modern thought.

A. THE DEVELOPMENT OF TEILHARD'S TELEOLOGY

Teilhard taught that man was *still* the center of the universe, as he held a special position in the evolutionary process. (In man both the internal and external structures of the universe are capable of direct investigation.) He taught that since man is the latest product of primate evolution he is of great biological significance. As a self-conscious being, man is qualitatively higher than all other biological species and therefore of great philosophical importance.

As a philosopher, Teilhard saw the universe as an unfolding process. All things were viewed correctly only if they were seen as parts of a universal Becoming. The old conceptions of a static, geocentric cosmology had misrepresented the organismic growth of the cosmos. Teilhard's new "vision" called for neologisms, and

---

[5]See in particular the fragments of Anaximander, Heraclitus, Empedocles, and also Lucretius' *On the Nature of Things,* Book V.

he wrote of a cosmogenesis which included a geogenesis, biogenesis, and noogenesis. The entire structure of the universe, from the stars to rational thought, represented a continuous process of development. Evolution was not merely a provisional and useful hypothesis, but a law covering all inorganic, organic, and psychic phenomena. And he held that he had discovered a law of evolution that gave meaning and purpose to the multiplicity of phenomena. A law which he taught not only explained the past history of the cosmos but, if extended to its final, logical conclusion, could also predict the condition of the ultimate earth and the end of planetary evolution. We shall see that he referred to it as the Law of Complexity-Consciousness. But to be more exact by taking into consideration the centralizing or converging nature of the evolving cosmos, he referred to it as the Law of centro-Complexity-Consciousness.

As a theologian, Teilhard sought to reconcile evolution with a personal God, the immortality of the human soul, and the freedom of the human will. He taught that theology, philosophy, and science were merely three distinct but not separate levels of investigation. Each presented one perspective of a single cosmic process. Each supplemented the others in giving a total, coherent view of man's place in the universe.

And as a mystic, Teilhard experienced the evolving unity of a spiritual universe; a cosmogenesis that was developing toward a Personal Center. But Teilhard never neglected science. It was through nature that he arrived at his mysticism, i.e. through evolution to God. At the end of the whole cosmic process, his mysticism taught that panentheism would be resolved in a true pantheism in which *"God shall be all in all."*[6]

Teilhard is concerned with the whole phenomenon of man, i.e. the unique appearance of man within the scheme of things. But every descriptive methodology necessarily implies an ontology; there is no inquiry free from presuppositions for they are either implicit or explicit. Therefore, although he claims to be giving merely a scientific description of evolution, we are not

------

[6]*The Phenomenon of Man*, p. 294. See also 262, 267, and 309-310 for further references to pantheism.

surprised when the Jesuit-priest ultimately grounds his view in theology.

What Teilhard does give us, at least in part, is a phenomenological interpretation of planetary evolution. Unlike Husserl's subjective methodology,[7] Teilhard's orientation is both subjective and objective in order to do justice to both interior or conscious as well as exterior or material evolution. His phenomenology is concerned with a descriptive analysis of the essential structures, relationships, and essences within the phenomena of planetary evolution. Without doing injustice to established facts, he wanted to reduce cosmic phenomena to their essential formations in order to establish a fundamental law that would disclose the meaning and purpose of evolution and man's place in the universe. It is unfortunate that in his phenomenological reduction of planetary evolution, Teilhard had not suspended his religious biases. His idealistic orientation is always present:

> We are seeking a qualitative law of development that from sphere to sphere should be capable of explaining, first of all the invisibility, then the appearance, and then the gradual dominance of the *within* in comparison to the *without* of things.[8]

After Bergson's profound influence on Teilhard, the latter accepted an evolutionary perspective.[9] In an early essay, "The Transformist Paradox" (1925), Teilhard wrote:

> Broadly understood, as it should be, transformism is now a hypothesis no longer. It has become the form of thought without which no scientific explanation is possible. That is why, even in an absolutely

---

[7]Marvin Farber advocates a broad but critical naturalism that incorporates the phenomenological method without adopting an idealistic ontology. See Marvin Farber: *The Aims of Phenomenology: The Motives, Methods, and Impact of Husserl's Thought.* New York, Harper and Row, 1966; *Phenomenology and Existence: Toward a Philosophy within Nature.* New York, Harper and Row, 1967; *Basic Issues of Philosophy: Experience, Reality, and Human Values.* New York, Harper and Row, 1968, and *Naturalism and Subjectivism.* Albany, State University of New York Press, 1968.

[8]*The Phenomenon of Man,* p. 61.

[9]It is interesting but strange to note that Teilhard never refers to Henri Bergson in *The Phenomenon of Man,* and seldom in all of his other writings. Bergson had been a tremendous influence on Teilhard, and their views have much in common.

unexpected form, it will inevitably continue to direct and animate the morphology of the future.[10]

For Teilhard, as for Spencer and Bergson, the evolutionary theory embraced inorganic, organic, and psychic phenomena. In fact, Teilhard held that only an evolutionary perspective provided the orientation from which the phenomena were rationally meaningful. In *The Phenomenon of Man* he clearly stated this position:

> Is evolution a theory, a system or a hypothesis? It is much more: it is a general condition to which all theories, all hypotheses, all systems must bow and which they must satisfy henceforward if they are to be thinkable and true. Evolution is a light illuminating all facts, a curve that all lines must follow.[11]

Later, in "Degrees of Scientific Certainty in the Idea of Evolution" (1946), he still held to this orientation:

> The idea of evolution: not, as is still sometimes said, a mere hypothesis, but a condition of all experience—or again, if you prefer the expression, the universal curve to which all our present and future ways of constructing the universe must henceforth conform, if they are to be scientifically valid or even thinkable.[12]

Most scientists and philosophers were to accept the evolutionary perspective. But Teilhard went further, holding that the entire universe manifested a cosmic design which gave purpose and a single direction to evolution in general, and the human phylum in particular. In "Cosmic Life" (1916) he wrote:

> We are all interconnected elements of one and the same curve that extends ahead of and reaches back behind us. . . . The analysis of matter is making us see it as a limitless aggregation of centres taking over and mastering one another in such a way as to build up, by their combination, more and more complex centres of a higher order.[13]

Besides Pascal's two abysses, the infinitely great and the infinitely small, Teilhard recognized and emphasized the evolution-

---

[10]*The Vision of the Past,* p. 87.
[11]*The Phenomenon of Man,* p. 219.
[12]*Science and Christ,* p. 193.
[13]*Writings in Time of War,* pp. 15, 19.

ary significance of a third abyss in the universe, that of infinite complexity in elemental arrangement. In "Creative Union" (1917) we have a clear statement of his position:

> . . . the universe is committed to *a Becoming* . . . *an absolute direction,* which is *towards Spirit.* . . . From the constitution of his protoplasm to his muscular and nervous tissue, the most spiritual being known to science—Man—is at the same time the being that is made up of the greatest number of parts. We may say that in our world psychic perfection varies in inverse[14] ratio with organic complexity and instability. . . . Soul, at all its degrees, was born of this progressive concentration of the primordial dust. . . . We may therefore conclude that if the most refined psychism coincides, in our universe, with the most complex material basis, then this is *by structural necessity.* . . . Thus, in the process of becoming, organic complexity and psychic simplicity are not in opposition: the one, in fact, is the condition for the appearance of the other.[15]

And elsewhere he wrote:

> From the smallest detail to the hugest concentration, *our living universe* (like our material universe) has a structure, and this structure can only be due to a phenomenon of growth.[16]
>
> Things have a definite direction. We are passing ahead, and we are making good progress.[17]

For Teilhard the universe may be viewed from two perspectives. From a synchronic or horizontal perspective we are impressed with the size of things. The objects of the universe display a tremendous range of size from the "parts" of the atoms to the immense stars and comets. In this range man is often held to occupy a position midway between the infinitely great and the infinitely small. As a result, his position in the scheme of things seems inconsequential. This, Teilhard holds, is our first observation but the conclusion is erroneous.

If we take a diachronic or vertical view of the universe, i.e. if we consider the position of things within the historical growth of the cosmos, then our first conclusion is radically changed for man becomes the most significant object in nature. This follows, Teil-

---

[14]Teilhard inadvertently wrote "inverse ratio" for "direct ratio."

[15]*Ibid.,* pp. 154, 155, 157.

[16]*The Vision of the Past,* p. 20.

[17]*Science and Christ,* p. 81.

hard taught, by observing the degree of interior complexity and resulting *radial* energy manifested in the sequential emergence of things. We have three general stages of evolution: pre-life, life, and thought. Within each stage there is great diversity. Yet, Teilhard observes, as we ascend the atoms of the periodic table and follow through organic and psycho-social evolution we find that each successive manifestation of evolution is more complex in the interior configuration of elements as well as manifesting greater degrees of *radial* energy. The simplest living things, e.g. viruses and bacteria, are infinitely more complex in their interior structure than the composition of stars and geological formations. Likewise, the metazoans are infinitely more complex than the protozoans, and the vertebrates are more complex than the invertebrates. As we move through the fishes, amphibians, reptiles, birds and mammals to the emergence of man, we notice that this natural tendency towards greater complexification continues but at an accelerated rate. According to Teilhard, the degree of consciousness is directly proportional to the degree of interior complexification and concentration, and determines the position of any object in the evolutionary scale of nature. Teilhard argues that man is the most significant creature in the universe because he is the most complex and therefore the most conscious. In fact, he is self-conscious. This anthropocentrism is unequivocal in his thought.

Teilhard taught that "to write the true natural history of the world, we should need to be able to follow it from *within*."[18] Therefore, to correlate this evolutionary increase of complexity or interiorization of "matter" with the resultant increase of psychic activity, he held that there must be "a certain law on which reality is built up, an hierarchical law of increasing complexity in unity."[19] He referred to this qualitative law or curve of the universe as the "cosmic" Law of centro-Complexity-Consciousness. The law provided a means for viewing geological, biological, and psycho-social evolution as three distinct stages of one con-

---

[18]*The Phenomenon of Man,* p. 151.
[19]*Science and Christ,* pp. 29-30.

tinuous process.[20] Likewise, the law provided Teilhard with an argument for order, direction, and purpose within evolution. He always held that "evolution has a precise *orientation* and a privileged *axis:*"[21]

> Leaving aside all anthropocentrism and anthropomorphism, I believe I can see a direction and a line of progress for life, a line and a direction which are in fact so well marked that I am convinced their reality will be universally admitted by the science of tomorrow.[22]
>
> From the cell to the thinking animal, as from the atom to the cell, a single process (a psychical kindling or concentration) goes on without interruption and always in the same direction.[23]

Teilhard noted that the primates were of special importance. During seventy million years of primate evolution we see the successive emergence of the Prosimians (treeshrew, lemur, loris, and tarsier), the Old World Monkeys (Cercopithecoidea or catarrhines) and New World Monkeys (Ceboidea or platyrrhines), and the great apes (gibbon, orangutan, chimpanzee, and gorilla). From the Miocene apes, the Dryopithecinae, emerged two distinct directions: (a) the line of Great Apes and (b) the line of primate evolution leading directly to man. Collectively these two directions represent the Hominoidea. Human evolution is represented by three successive stages: (a) the Australopithecinae, (b) the Pithecanthropoids, and (c) the Neanderthaloids. In short, hominid evolution is represented by *Homo robustus, Homo erec-*

---

[20]Teilhard saw the Law of Complexity-Consciousness manifested in the successive developments of planetary evolution: units of psychic energy (stuff of the universe); elementary corpuscles, e.g. protons, neutrons, electrons, and photons; atoms, molecules, mega-molecules; and cells, i.e. protozoans and metazoans. In organic evolution the acceleration of the law becomes obvious as we move up through the fishes, amphibians, reptiles, birds and mammals, to man. The acceleration of complexification has concentrated in the differentiation of nervous tissue and the increase of brain size. Teilhard saw the plant and insect kingdoms as unsuccessful deviations from this general tendency. He held that the insects, particularly the Hymenoptera and Lepidoptera orders, represented great diversity and complexity but their *radial* energy had been ossified as instinct. And the psychism in plants is very diffuse.

[21]*The Phenomenon of Man*, p. 142.

[22]*Ibid.*

[23]*Ibid.*, p. 169.

tus, and *Homo sapiens* respectively.[24] Teilhard notes that from the evolution of the treeshrew to *Homo sapiens,* the Law of centro-Complexity-Consciousness accelerated rapidly, concentrating on the nervous system and brain:

> What makes the primates so interesting and important to biology is, in the first place, that they represent a phylum of pure and direct cerebralisation. . . . In the case of the primates, on the other hand, evolution went straight to work on the brain, neglecting everything else, which accordingly remained malleable. That is why they are at the head of the upward and onward march towards greater consciousness. In this singular and privileged case, the particular orthogenesis of the phylum happened to coincide exactly with the principal orthogenesis of life itself.[25]

The continued acceleration of the Law of centro-Complexity-Consciousness within the human phylum was held to be responsible for the emergence of "the central phenomenon, *reflection.*"[26] Teilhard argued that from a planetary perspective the future outcome of this phenomenon could only be a super-conscious collectivity of reflective persons. In "Degrees of Scientific Certainty in the Idea of Evolution" (1946) he wrote:

> In conformity with the law of complexity-consciousness, what, in fact, we are witnessing throughout the whole of human history is an ultra-synthesis directed towards grouping in some super-organism of a completely new type, not atoms, now, or molecules, or cells, but in-

---

[24]For a recent clear but brief introduction to the evidence supporting human evolution and its interpretation see C. Loring Brace: *The Stages of Human Evolution.* Englewood Cliffs, New Jersey, Prentice-Hall, 1967.

[25]*The Phenomenon of Man,* pp. 159-160. Although we may be impressed with the size of the dinosaurs which dominated the earth for over one hundred million years during the Mesozoic era, they had incredibly small brains. Teilhard speaks of cephalization and cerebralization. By cephalization he refers to the general increase of the size of the brain. Cerebralization refers to the increase of the size of the cerebrum. The frontal lobes of the cerebrum are necessary for abstract thinking. Primate evolution is important because it manifests a rapid increase in the size of the brain in general and in the size of the cerebrum in particular. The average cranial capacity of the gorilla is 500 c.c., while the average volume of the human brain is 1500 c.c. But Teilhard held that man's superior intelligence is not only due to the fact that his brain is triple in size when compared to the gorilla's, but more importantly that its neural structure is infinitely more complex.

[26]*Ibid.,* p. 165.

dividuals and even complete phyla. In other words, mankind, in process of collectivisation around us, represents, I suggest, from the Scientific point of view, the appearance in the universe of some supercomplex.[27]

In "Some Reflections on Progress" (1941), Teilhard generalized the position he had formulated in his recently completed *The Phenomenon of Man:*

Let me here repeat the two fundamental equations or equivalents which we have established:
Progress = growth of consciousness.
Growth of Consciousness = effect of organisation.[28]

And in "Life and the Planets: What is Happening at this Moment on Earth?" (1945), he wrote:

So it comes to this, that when we have reached the point where complexity can no longer be reckoned in number of atoms we can nevertheless continue to measure it (and accurately) by noting the increase of consciousness in the living creature—in practical terms, the development of its nervous system. This is the solution of our problem.[29]

Teilhard never deviated from his spiritualistic and teleological orientation. In "The Formation of the Noosphere: A Biological Interpretation of Human History" (1947), he wrote:

Complexification due to the growth of consciousness, or consciousness the outcome of complexity: experimentally the two terms are inseparable.[30]

---

[27]*Science and Christ,* p. 195. Teilhard referred to the fundamental "groping" of evolution toward higher syntheses within a precise orientation and toward a specific target, i.e. a final, ultimate synthesis or the unity of the universe with God, as a process of "directed chance." Although he was aware of the influences of the environment and biological mutations on the process of evolution, he held that from a cosmic perspective the whole process revealed a direction too obvious to be merely the result of cumulative chance variations. By neglecting these influences, and maintaining that *tangential* energy is determined while *radial* energy is free, he has not resolved the problem of freedom and determinism. He holds that the universe through evolution is increasing in freedom. But did he not maintain that the universe *is* ultimately this free psychic energy?

[28]Pierre Teilhard de Chardin: *The Future of Man.* New York, Harper and Row, 1964, p. 69.

[29]*Ibid.,* pp. 111-112.

[30]*Ibid.,* p. 174.

Teilhard held to this historico-phenomenological distinction, but grounded it in monism. The dualism in Teilhard's thought is merely epistemological.

The "cosmic" Law of centro-Complexity-Consciousness is as crucial to Teilhard's thought as is his spiritual monism. For Teilhard desires to make a leap of faith from the allegedly rational order of cosmic evolution to the existence of a Supreme Intelligence, i.e. from the design in the universe to an Absolute Mind. He never doubted that evolution revealed such a design. In "A Defence of Orthogenesis in the Matter of Patterns of Speciation" (1955), an essay written only three months before his death, he still held to teleology:

> A general drift of complexity/consciousness drawing the corpuscular stuff of the universe globally (whatever its diversification of detail) towards ever more improbable states of organization and interiorization. . . . Willingly or unwillingly, paleontology is, and cannot help becoming increasingly the *science of orthogenesis,* which it must consider both in its general, fundamental drift and in the various branches into which it divides in the course of its route.[31]

He saw psycho-social evolution as the continuation of biological evolution. The law of increased complexity now manifested itself in technological development. He held that for the most part man has remained biologically stable for the last thirty thousand years. His body, except for a large brain, has remained relatively unspecialized. The innovation of tool-making was analogous to a favorable biological mutation.[32] For over two million years man has used tools, whether they be of bone, teeth, antler, stone, or metal. Teilhard saw tools as specialized extensions of the human body with which man could adapt the environment to suit his needs and interests. During the last thirty thousand years the acceleration of complexity in tools has been mirrored in the increased complexity of man's social structures.

---

[31]*The Vision of the Past,* p. 273.

[32]The behavioral gap between the great apes and man has been further narrowed by the recent discovery that chimpanzees in their natural habitat are toolmakers as well as tool-users, although only man is presently capable of using simple tools to make more complex instruments. See Jane van Lawick-Goodall, *In the Shadow of Man* (Boston: Houghton Mifflin Company, 1971).

Although man's social structures have their origins with the earlier primates,[33] his superior intelligence has allowed him to become increasingly capable of directing his own further evolution.

Teilhard always remained optimistic. He even held that wars were merely the growing pains of a converging human evolution.[34] With the continued increase of the human population on the closed surface of the earth accompanied with the further acceleration of technology, he envisioned a psychically unified earth as the final synthesis of complexity-consciousness.[35] That is, the formation of a super-consciousness of persons as the final result of the evolutionary concentration of a monadic universe. In the last analysis, Teilhard held the "Great Chain of Being" to be a natural scale of increasing complexity and consciousness ranging from the homogeneous units of the universe to the ultra-complexity of the future.

Lastly, Teilhard's Law of centro-Complexity-Consciousness may be considered a dialectical process as long as one remains merely concerned with the phenomena of cosmic evolution. There is a direct relationship between "matter" and psychic energy in their historical development. Likewise, we shall see that Teilhard does maintain that increased quantitative changes in evolution do eventually result in qualitative changes. (Hegel had held the dialectical process to be eternal, whereas Teilhard's view of evolution is finalistic.)

B. TELEOLOGY IN THE EVOLUTIONARY LITERATURE

Among the evolutionists, Lamarck, Spencer, Wallace, Fiske, Nietzsche, Haeckel, Bergson, Alexander, Sellars, Smuts, and Mor-

---

[33]For recent studies on primate behavior see Desmond Morris: *Primate Ethology*. Chicago, Aldine, 1967; Vernon Reynolds: *The Apes*. New York, Dutton, 1967; and Irven DeVore (Ed.): *Primate Behavior*. New York, Holt, Rinehart and Winston, 1965.

[34]Teilhard simply rejected the possibility that human evolution could be aborted by a global catastrophe.

[35]How impressed Teilhard would be if he had lived to see the computerization of modern society. No doubt he would have interpreted it as a further step toward global unity.

gan were also aware of the general trend in evolution from the simpler to the more complex.

Lamarck's interpretation of evolution was anthropocentric as he had maintained that man is the most perfect of animals and therefore is the standard from which all other animals are judged. He saw evolution as a linear succession, but represented it as a degradation in complexity of organization, intelligence, and number of faculties. Man represented the most perfect animal while the protozoans were the simplest and therefore the most imperfect:

> It may then be truly said that in each kingdom of living bodies the groups are arranged in a single graduated series, in conformity with the increasing complexity of organisation and the affinities of the object. . . . Thus if the most perfect animals are at one extremity of the chain, the opposite extremity will necessarily be occupied by the simplest and most imperfect animals found in nature.[36]

In biological evolution Lamarck did distinguish between (a) the grand linear series of organisms from the simple and imperfect to the complex and perfect without gaps[37] and (b) particular series of evolutions resulting in the small, collateral, branching networks of species.[38] Although Lamarck did not formulate a cosmic law of evolution as Teilhard has done, he did recognize the relationship between biological complexity and mental faculties.

Spencer did formulate a cosmic law of cyclical evolution. He held that the evolution from the homogeneous to the heterogeneous was necessary and universal, and encompassed the inorganic, organic, and psycho-social levels of development:

> The advance from the simple to the complex, through a process of successive differentiations, is seen alike in the earliest changes of the Universe to which we can reason our way back, and in the earliest changes which we can inductively establish; it is seen in the geologic

---

[36]Lamarck: *Zoological Philosophy*, pp. 59, 68.

[37]Lamarck denied that there had been the extinction of any biological species, for he assumed that any gaps in the continuous chain of evolution were merely due to the lack of evidence. Compare with Aristotle.

[38]Teilhard had also distinguished between the general direction of planetary evolution due to the Law of centro-Complexity-Consciousness and the ramifications found at each level, e.g. the branching or fanning out of particular biological species.

and climatic evolution of the Earth, and of every single organism on its surface; it is seen in the evolution of Humanity, whether contemplated in the civilized individual, or in the aggregations of races; it is seen in the evolution of Society, in respect alike of its political, its religious, and its economical organization; and it is seen in the evolution of all those endless concrete and abstract products of human activity, which constitute the environment of our daily life. From the remotest past which Science can fathom, up to the novelties of yesterday, an essential trait of Evolution has been the transformation of the homogeneous into the heterogeneous. . . . Universally, then, the effect is more complex than the cause.[39]

We have seen that Spencer neither established a spiritualistic monism nor argued that his cosmic law would terminate in a final state of universal complexity. The Force of evolution originates from the Unknowable, while the cosmos repeats its cyclical pattern ad infinitum.

Alfred Russel Wallace, unlike Darwin, had given evolution a spiritualistic interpretation. His views are personal impressions rather than developed philosophical arguments. Like Spencer, he held that matter is Force. But Wallace further maintained, like Teilhard, that Force was ultimately spiritual in nature:

. . . matter is essentially force, and nothing but force; that matter, as popularly understood, does not exist, and is, in fact, philosophically inconceivable. . . . It does not seem an improbable conclusion that all force may be will-force; and thus, that the whole universe, is not merely dependent on, but actually *is*, the WILL of higher intelligences or of one Supreme Intelligence.[40]

And in his work on Darwinism he concluded:

These three distinct stages of progress from the inorganic world of matter and motion up to man, point clearly to an unseen universe—to a world of spirit, to which the world of matter is altogether subordinate. . . . We, who accept the existence of a spiritual world, can look upon the universe as a grand consistent whole adapted in all its parts to the development of spiritual beings capable of indefinite life and perfectibility.[41]

[39]Spencer: *First Principles*, pp. 358-359, 429.

[40]Alfred Russel Wallace: *Contributions to the Theory of Natural Selection.* New York, Macmillan, 1870, pp. 365-366, 368. See pp. 363-371.

[41]Alfred Russel Wallace: *Darwinism: An Exposition of the Theory of Natural Selection with Some of its Applications.* London, Macmillan, 1923, pp. 476, 477.

Now Teilhard had maintained that the human soul is a natural product of biological evolution, although we shall see that he likewise gives a natural argument for its immortality. Wallace, even though holding the universe to be spiritualistic, does not maintain that the human soul is the product of increased complexity. He argues that its immortality demonstrates the existence of a Supreme Intelligence, the latter being responsible for man's superior mental abilities:

> But this greater and greater complexity, even if carried to an infinite extent, cannot, of itself, have the slightest tendency to originate consciousness in such molecules or groups of molecules. If a material element, or a combination of a thousand material elements in a molecule, are alike unconscious, it is impossible for us to believe, that the mere addition of one, two, or a thousand other material elements to form a more complex molecule, could in any way tend to produce a self-conscious existence. The things are radically distinct.[42]

Where Teilhard's law of evolution is an attempt to reconcile material complexity with the emergence of self-consciousness, Wallace held to the traditional dualistic interpretation even though he did acknowledge the direction toward greater complexity in biological evolution. (In his last writings Wallace did advocate a spiritualistic monism.)

Fiske's *Cosmic Philosophy* continued to reinstate Spencer's *Synthetic Philosophy,* the former referring to the latter's discovery of a cosmic law of evolution to be as great an intellectual achievement as Newton's discovery of the law of gravitation:

> . . . Spencer's discovery is on a par with Newton's. . . . Unavoidably, in using the word Evolution, we have suggested the idea of increase in structural complexity. . . . In short, in a survey of the whole organic world, progress from lower to higher forms is a progress from forms which are less, to forms which are more, differentiated and integrated.[43]

Even Friedrich Nietzsche, when preparing his notes for his book, *The Eternal Recurrence,* remarked that evolution displays

---

[42]Wallace: *Contributions to the Theory of Natural Selection,* p. 365.

[43]Fiske: *Outlines of Cosmic Philosophy Based on the Doctrine of Evolution, with Criticisms on the Positive Philosophy.* vol. 2, pp. 205-206, 211, 238.

"the simplest forms striving toward the most complex."[44] However, Spencer, Fiske, and Nietzsche held that each evolutionary ascent ended in a degeneration of forms from the most complex to the simplest. Teilhard, always concerned with eschatology, held that planetary evolution ended with the attainment of the most concentrated state of complexity-consciousness.

Haeckel wrote in his *Last Words on Evolution* (1905) that:

> . . . the more complex species have been evolved from a series of simpler forms according to Darwinian principles. . . . The fishes, dipneusts, amphibians, reptiles, monotremes, marsupials, placentals, lemurs, apes, anthropoid apes, and ape-men (pithecanthropi), are inseparable links of a long ancestral chain, of which the last and most perfect link is man.[45]

Haeckel's position is not meant to imply anthropocentrism, a doctrine which he rejected. He merely acknowledged that in the long series of biological organisms that have evolved, man *is* the most complex, and that degrees of sensitivity are directly related to the degree of complexity in the neural structure and brain. Therefore, since man's nervous system and brain are the most complex in the animal kingdom, it is not surprising that he should manifest the greatest degree of consciousness. In fact, man is self-conscious as a result of his biological structure.

Bergson had also held to the direct relationship between matter and consciousness. There was no matter without some degree of consciousness, and likewise no consciousness without a material foundation. Evolution was, in fact, increasing complexity and consciousness manifested within the diversity of plants, insects, and animals. In *Creative Evolution* (1907) he wrote:

> Experience, then, shows that the most complex has been able to issue from the most simple by way of evolution. . . . The increasing complexity of the organism is therefore due theoretically (in spite of innumerable exceptions due to accidents of evolution) to the necessity of complexity in the nervous system.[46]

---

[44]Nietzsche: *The Will to Power*, p. 550.

[45]Ernst Haeckel: *Last Words on Evolution*. New York, Eckler, 1905, pp. 61, 97. Haeckel's hypothesis that the "missing link" would be found in Asia inspired his student, Eugene Dubois, to travel to Java where he subsequently discovered *Pithecanthropus erectus* (1890-1892).

[46]Bergson: *Creative Evolution*, pp. 28, 274.

But Bergson's metaphysics of evolution, we have seen, rests upon an ontological dualism. Ultimate reality is (a) the creative stream of consciousness or *élan vital* running through the (b) inert matter of the universe. In man, the two aspects are united through the activity of perception. Teilhard, however, rejected dualism in favor of monism. A dualism in nature would never have given the Jesuit-priest the ultimate unity he envisioned as the final goal of a converging, spiritualistic cosmogenesis.

The emergent evolutionists saw the increase of complexity resulting in the emergence of new qualities or properties. Alexander wrote:

> The higher emergent has been described as based on a complexity of the lower existents; thus life is a complex of material bodies and mind of living ones. Ascent takes place, it would seem, through complexity. But at each change of quality the complexity as it were gathers itself together and is expressed in a new simplicity.[47]

And Sellars:

> We have already seen that the principle of evolution has now a practically universal application. It applies to suns and solar systems, to the chemical elements, to cultures, to nations. But there is another principle which goes with it and which it in a manner presupposes, the *principle of organization*.[48]

The evolutionists did not always speak of complexity or consciousness. Smuts spoke of the evolution of *wholes;* creative reality is caused by the continued production of new wholes from pre-existing wholes:

> Thus arise the physical, chemical, organic, psychical and personal categories, which are all expressive of holistic activity at its various levels and reducible to terms of Holism. . . . Thus mind structures presuppose life structures, and life structures presuppose energy structures, which are themselves graded according to the various forms of physical and chemical grouping.[49]

---

[47]Alexander: *Space, Time, and Deity*, vol. 2, p. 70.

[48]Sellars: *The Principles and Problems of Philosophy*, p. 274. It is unfortunate that Sellars never developed his *principle of organization* within a systematic explanation of emergent evolution.

[49]Smuts: *Holism and Evolution*, pp. 143, 169-170.

We may safely assume that the successive stages of physico-chemical, vital, mental, and personal structures manifest increased complexity. We shall see that Smuts' concern for the evolutionary significance of personality is also shared by Teilhard. (Teilhard taught of a personalizing universe and the ultra-personalization of man.)

In *The Emergence of Novelty* (1933), Morgan stressed the significance of organization:

> What we find throughout nature is advance in organization. . . Evolution thus offers a scientific interpretation of the advance of natural organization. . . . Hence it seems that precedence should now be given to organism rather than to mechanism—to organization rather than to aggregation.[50]

Teilhard did give preference to organism and organization, for he taught that the cosmos was like an organism developing in complexity and consciousness and stressed organization which he referred to as complexification. He clearly points out that by complexification he does not merely mean the aggregation or addition of more elements, but an increase in the interior complexity of organization.

C. FINAL INTERPRETATION

All of the philosophers of evolution have been aware that evolution displays a chain of products ranging from the simple to the more complex. Herbert Spencer had even formulated a cosmic Law to account for this trend. In his historico-phenomenological study of evolution, Teilhard has reduced the process to the fundamental "cosmic" Law of centro-Complexity-Consciousness. But there are serious errors in this interpretation.

The law, in fact, is not cosmic because Teilhard's perspective is not cosmic but *planetary*. To date there is no scientific evidence that biological and psycho-social evolution have, are, or will take place elsewhere in the solar system or universe. It is possible but not probable that evolution as it has taken place on the earth has occurred in the identical manner elsewhere. The number of vari-

---

[50]Morgan: *The Emergence of Novelty*, pp. 15, 16, 58.

ables involved that would have to be duplicated exactly in the same sequence staggers the imagination (one recalls Nietzsche's doctrine of Eternal Recurrence). Man may prove to be the only rational being in the universe. The only evolutionary process that Teilhard was knowledgeable of is the one that is occurring on this planet. Likewise, it is merely assumptive reasoning to hold that evolution *must* always result in greater complexity-consciousness. Plants, insects, and other orders of animals have evolved without displaying a tendency towards self-consciousness. In short, increased consciousness is not *always* the necessary result of increased complexity. Teilhard has generally ignored the evolution of plants and insects because of his anthropocentric orientation. Bergson's creative but divergent philosophy of evolution is less dogmatic and less anthropocentric in that it includes recognition of these other two major directions. Man is not, as Teilhard held, indispensable if we assume that he is the product of chance variations in an eternal and infinite universe. The plants and/or insects may yet inherit the earth.

Teilhard dealt with empirical description. As such, his alleged cosmic Law is actually an *a posteriori* tendency in nature rather than an *a priori* Law of the cosmos. It is a synthetic generalization limited to a planetary perspective. (One recalls Alfred North Whitehead's "Fallacy of Misplaced Concreteness." A crucial distinction is needed between idealizations and physical reality.) The extreme complexity of nature and the probability that nature in part or as a whole may evolve into a plurality of new structures within limitless space and time make the establishment of an *a priori* cosmic Law of process impossible. In short, there is no empirical guarantee that the end of the earth from a human perspective will result in the formation of an ultracomplex and superconscious entity.

Teilhard's value judgments are dogmatic and anthropocentric. According to his Law, something increases in value as it increases in complexity-consciousness. Man is held to be the most valuable object in the universe because he is the most complex and conscious animal. But we may value something for a plurality of reasons, e.g. its necessity, simplicity, practicality, beauty, uniqueness, etc.

Evolution is not synonymous with progress. Distinctions are called for. The present situation of the earth clearly demonstrates that technological progress is no guarantee of moral progress.

Finally, a general tendency in nature does not constitute proof of a pre-established design in cosmic or planetary evolution.[51] Biological evolution is a very inefficient process (most biological mutations are deleterious). Likewise, one would have to prove that this evolution is the best of all possible evolutions.

In short, to infer from the present data that evolution is the result of a Supreme Mind is to make an unwarranted leap from science to theology.

---

[51]See, George Gaylord Simpson: *Horses*. New York, Doubleday, 1961. The evolution of the horse during the sixty million years of the Cenozoic Era is often given as a classic example of orthogenetic descent. The generic series represented by *Hyracotherium* or *Eohippus, Orohippus, Epihippus, Mesohippus, Miohippus, Parahippus, Merychippus, Phiohippus,* and *Equus* are held by some to illustrate directional and purposeful evolution. But Simpson's book clearly shows that the evolution of the horse does not represent straight-line descent but multidirectional, adaptive radiation. The increase in the size and structure of the horse can be sufficiently accounted for within the principles of the synthetic theory of evolution. This conclusion is applicable to other species of plants and animals. Human culture also performs an adaptive function; there may or there may not be long-range goals present.

Chapter IV

TEILHARD'S CRITICAL THRESHOLDS

T HE PROPER conception of the nature of man and his place in the universe is crucial to the philosophical quest for truths. A true philosophical anthropology requires a rigorous science-oriented ontology and cosmology. However, it is unfortunate that many exponents of an alleged philosophical anthropology have little or no scientific evidence to justify their conceptions of man. Limiting inquiry to a single method or disregarding the established facts of the special sciences when formulating a philosophy of man is unforgivable. A myopic view yields unwarranted assumptions resulting in an untenable position concerning man's true place in the universe. A true philosophical anthropology must first consider the established facts of the natural and social sciences if it is to be at all meaningful. A cosmic and evolutionary perspective is also indispensable in relating man to the rest of nature. No other single orientation has been able to logically incorporate all known phenomena into a coherent, spatiotemporal sequence.

It was to Teilhard's credit that he had mastered and organized such a wide breadth of knowledge from the natural and social sciences. His twenty years of academic and social isolation in China were beneficial not only in providing opportunities for geological and paleontological research, but also in giving him ample time in which to do a vast amount of reading, reflection, and writing.[1]

Whatever Teilhard's shortcomings in his interpretations of the facts, his inquiry into the nature of man had the advantage of being, at least to a significant extent, scientific in approach. No other philosopher of evolution in the twentieth century can match Teilhard's extensive scientific training, research, and ex-

---

[1]For a partial list of Teilhard's readings while in Peking see Cuénot's *Teilhard de Chardin: A Biographical Study*, pp. 236-237.

perience. Not even Bergson was as competent in biology. In fact, Bergson had eschewed geology and paleontology in favor of an intuitional approach to the metaphysical inquiry of time or duration. But Teilhard has unfortunately separated man from the rest of nature through the use of an unwarranted assumption, i.e. by maintaining that the progress of planetary evolution has crossed a series of critical thresholds that have resulted in the formation of new kinds of phenomena. This assumption is also theologically oriented, for Teilhard will rely upon it as an argument for the immortality of the human soul.

One need only walk through a large museum or zoo to become impressed with the great diversity and complexity of life on the earth. It is even more amazing when one realizes that this represents but an infinitely small part of all the living forms that have resulted from a biological process that has taken place for over three billion years. Yet one also becomes aware of the similarities between the vast array of forms. Within the primate order no two forms are so dissimilar that one cannot imagine that, with the proper genetic modifications and environmental changes as well as enough time, the simpler form could develop into the more complex.[2] An objective observer will admit that the great apes, especially the chimpanzee and gorilla, are biologically more similar to man than they are to the monkeys, i.e. they represent a "link" between man and the Old World Monkeys.[3] In short, there is no scientific evidence justifying an ontological separation between the apes and man. There are no ontological separations in the evolutionary process, merely distinctions due to natural differences. This, however, is not the position taken by Teilhard.

---

[2]This is an oversimplification of a very complex natural process, but the implication is clear and valid. The present understanding of genetics has made it possible for man to artificially produce variations in plants and animals. In the distant future, further genetic understanding will allow man to manipulate and/or select desired genes, enabling him to preprogram the characteristics and guide the embryonic development of humans. The moral questions that will arise are staggering—but so are the benefits. Teilhard favored eugenics, but never developed an ethical position. His understanding of population genetics was negligible.

[3]The great apes have also evolved during the past two million years. But their changes have been less significant because their habitats have remained relatively stable.

For he desired man to partake in a higher level of Becoming or Cosmogenesis. Once again, theological assumptions have undermined scientific evidence.

A. THE DEVELOPMENT OF TEILHARD'S EVOLUTIONARY SPHERES

Unlike Leibniz, Teilhard's cosmology does not advocate that nature is ultimately an unbroken continuum of psychic development.[4] For Teilhard, planetary evolution revealed four separate stages: (a) the stuff of the universe; (b) pre-life or sub-life; (c) life; (d) thought or reflection. (A fifth and final stage or event of directed evolution is held to be the union or synthesis of collective thought with a personal God.)

At the end of each successive stage of evolution a critical value is reached. At this single point in evolution there occurs a sudden or spontaneous change of state (aspect, condition, or nature), i.e. a critical point (threshold, level, or phase) is reached and as a direct result evolution takes a sudden leap forward and upward.[5] Each critical threshold is crossed once and only once. The result has been a series of successive layers (zones, spheres, envelopes, or orders), each layer differing from the previous layer not merely in its *degree* of psychic development, but in *kind*. The crossing of a critical threshold results in a qualitative change while a spectrum of quantitative differences is manifested within each level, e.g. each living organism manifests its own particular *degree* of psychic development according to its position in the evolutionary hierarchy, while man's psychic energy is held to differ in *kind*

---

[4]Leibniz's expression was *"Natura non fecit saltus;"* he referred to it as his Principle of Continuity.

[5]Although Teilhard held that each critical threshold was crossed instantly and only once, it is wrong to interpret him as believing in spontaneous generation. For it is one thing to maintain, as Teilhard did, that the first manifestations of pre-life, life, and thought were instantaneous, and quite another to hold that complex biological organisms have originated spontaneously from inorganic matter. The latter position was held by early biologists. The experiments of Pasteur helped to discredit the position. It should be noted that the cosmozoic theory, i.e. the position that life reached the earth from another sphere, is not supported by scientific evidence. See A. I. Oparin: *The Origin of Life.* New York, Dover, 1953.

since he belongs to a new and higher level of existence, i.e. the sphere of thought.

The total evolution of the earth has thus far manifested three unique events. The first critical threshold occurred at the *granulation* of the stuff of the universe or psychic units of energy, resulting in the sudden formation of elementary corpuscles represented by protons, neutrons, electrons, and photons, etc. Further evolution resulted in crystallization and polymerization; atoms, molecules, and mega-molecules were formed.

The second critical threshold distinguishes between the inorganic level or *pre-biosphere* and the formation of a living level or biosphere. A qualitative leap from units of pre-living atoms to units of living cells had taken place. Teilhard held that organic evolution is qualitatively different from and higher than inorganic evolution, for organic evolution is not only homogeneous and coherent but manifests the emergence of new kinds of phenomena which he refers to as elementary movements of life: reproduction, multiplication or duplication, renovation or diversification or ramification, conjugation, association or aggregation, controlled additivity. In organic evolution the phenomenon of controlled additivity acts as a vertical component, and is responsible for biological evolution *"in a pre-determined direction."*[6] Thus, as a result of controlled complication or orthogenesis,[7] the living system of the planet results in a hierarchy in which:

> . . . terms *succeed each other* experimentally, following constantly increasing degrees of centro-complexity. . . . Without orthogenesis life would only have spread; with it there is an ascent of life that is invincible. . . . By the force of orthogenesis the individual unit becomes part of a chain.[8]

In general, Teilhard held that life manifests groping profusion, constructive ingenuity, and indifference. Yet it structurally formed a *global unity.* And he saw the solidarity of organic evolution as "one single and gigantic organism:"

---

[6]*The Phenomenon of Man,* p. 108.

[7]Orthogenesis infers directional development. For Teilhard, it means evolution in the direction of greater complexity-consciousness.

[8]*Ibid.,* pp. 108, 109, 111.

> To see life properly we must never lose sight of the unity of the
> biopshere that lies beyond the plurality and essential rivalry of
> individual beings.[9]

The crossing of the last critical threshold resulted in the qualitative distinction between life and thought. In short, we have the emergence, vitalization, and hominization of "matter" or, to be more Teilhardian, psychic or *radial* energy. As a product of evolution:

> Man is unable to see himself entirely unrelated to mankind, neither
> is he able to see mankind unrelated to life, nor life unrelated to the
> universe.[10]

With man we have the emergence of a new and higher kind of phenomenon, reflection or awareness *in the second degree:*

> After the grain of matter, the grain of life; and now at last we see
> constituted the *grain of thought*.[11]

Atoms, cells, and persons represent the building blocks of these three successive stages of planetary evolution respectively. And with the emergence of man we have the formation of:

> . . . a region endowed with extraordinary properties forming a new
> and independent zone of the universe, and yet produced, in some
> way, by the maturing of the entire earth. . . . Humanity is not out-
> side life but extends the line of life. Man is momentarily a *climax*
> in the universe; and a leading shoot also, to the extent that by his
> intense psychism he confirms the reality and fixes the direction of
> a rise of consciousness through things.[12]

The emergence of man as a reflective animal represented a unique cosmic event. Teilhard taught that man is not only the last-born, freshest, most complex, conscious, elastic, and subtle of all animals, but, and of infinitely more importance, he constitutes the axis of evolution pointing the way to the final unification of the world in terms of life.

Also crucial to Teilhard's philosophy of evolution is the finite spherical surface of the earth. This factor prevents the indefinite

---

[9]*Ibid.,* p. 112.
[10]*Ibid.,* p. 34.
[11]*Ibid.,* p. 173.
[12]*The Vision of the Past,* pp. 52, 58, 229.

dispersion of each distinct evolutionary layer. Pre-life, life, and thought are able to converge or involute about the planet. As a result of the *law of succession*[13] and the finite sphericity of the earth, Teilhard abstracts superimposed but coextensive planetary circles or envelopes, each successive envelope differing in *kind* from the previous one. From this perspective of a converging evolution, we have the successive formations of the geosphere,[14] biosphere,[15] and noosphere; inorganic, organic, and reflective envelopes respectively. Each sphere represents a distinct stage of cosmogenesis, for the axis of geogenesis was extended in biogenesis which now is expressing itself in noogenesis or psycho-social evolution.

From Teilhard's position cosmogenesis cannot be represented as a continuum. There are sudden leaps which represent gaps in nature.[16] This position is not in accordance with the implications of scientific evidence.[17]

Now as a direct result of evolution having crossed the third and latest critical threshold, Teilhard maintained that man differs in *kind,* not merely in *degree,* from the other earlier animals, e.g. the great apes which man is biologically closest to phylogenetically. With the emergence of man, planetary evolution took a qualitative leap forward and upward. And because of the finite surface of the earth, man has been able to evolve collectively. He has formed a psychosocial layer or thinking envelope around the planet—the noosphere. The theological significance of maintain-

---

[13]Refers to the necessary qualitative leaps in evolution when energy has reached a certain critical point of internal concentration. Contrast with Darwin.

[14]Includes the barysphere, lithosphere, hydrosphere, atmosphere, and stratosphere.

[15]Includes the plant, insect, and animal worlds.

[16]In Teilhard's historico-phenomenological analysis of converging evolution, the geosphere, biosphere, and noosphere represent the successive essential structures of planetary development.

[17]Thre is no need to assume gaps within the evolution of the planet. Just as the protozoans, e.g. the *euglena,* infer a common evolutionary origin of the plant and animal kingdoms, so the viruses represent a "link" between the pre-living and living worlds. Changing environmental conditions are responsible for destroying evidence. Man's classification of nature must be diachronic as well as synchronic if it is not to be deceptive.

ing a critical threshold between the other primates and man is
explicit in the following quotes from Teilhard:

> Until man appeared upon earth, the fountain of life rose up before
> the Creator, smooth and straight, in the transparence of a single
> coherent effort. Obediently applying themselves to the task of repro-
> ducing and improving themselves, the lower animal forms were un-
> swerving in their pursuit of the synthesis, within them, of spirit.
> . . . Instantly, there was a change in the apparent texture of life.
> . . . Man, through his spiritual soul, steps up into a new ontologi-
> cal and biological level. . . . Between the perishable souls of animals
> and man's immortal spirit, there is not exactly a hiatus: there is a
> transition from one to the other through a critical point. . . . The
> appearance of the human soul, as an autonomous and indestructible
> element of the world, is the supreme example of these levels of in-
> determination in the evolution of our cosmos. With man, we reach
> the end of one particular plane—a circle is drawn around the uni-
> verse.[18]

From a zoological point of view,[19] man represented for Teilhard "the vertebrate, the mammal, the living being, *par excel-
lence.*"[20] But ontologically, Teilhard held that man represented a
"critical point . . . a change of state, a break" in the continuum
of life:[21]

> Man is an embarrassment to science only because it hesitates to ac-
> cept him at his full significance, that is to say as the appearance, at
> the goal of a continuous transformation, of an absolutely new state of
> life. Let us recognize frankly, once and for all, that in any realistic
> picture of world history, the coming to power of thought is as real,
> specific, and great an event as the first condensation of matter or
> the first appearance of life: and we shall perhaps see, instead of the
> disorder we feared, a more perfect harmony pervading our picture
> of the universe.[22]

In reality, another world is born. Abstraction, logic, reasoned choice

---

[18]*Writings in Time of War*, pp. 104, 64, 157, 252. Note the orthogenetic and
teleological interpretation of biological evolution.

[19]For a recent but controversial study of the nature of man, see Desmond Morris: *The Naked Ape: A Zoologist's Study of the Human Animal.* New York, Mc-
Graw-Hill, 1967, and *The Human Zoo.* New York, McGraw-Hill, 1969.

[20]*The Vision of the Past*, p. 73.

[21]*Ibid.*, pp. 166, 167.

[22]*Ibid.*, p. 167.

and inventions, mathematics, art, calculation of space and time, anxieties and dreams of love—all these activities of *inner life* are nothing else than the effervescence of the newly-formed centre as it explodes onto itself.[23]

From an evolutionary perspective that extends into the billions of years, man has emerged relatively recently from his common ancestry with the great apes.[24] Like Nietzsche, Teilhard held that man is still incomplete, i.e. unfinished in actualizing his evolutionary potentialities.

To properly evaluate man's *natural* position in the cosmos and anticipate his planetary destiny, Teilhard held that it was "necessary and sufficient to consider the *within* as well as the *without* of things."[25] From *without* man has acquired an erect position, larger brain,[26] and the ability to make tools. From *within*, which for Teilhard reveals the accurate measure of qualitative development, man represents a unique phenomenon in the universe. For the first and only time in biological evolution and *at one single stroke*, the development of *radial* energy had taken an infinite leap forward and upward resulting in a chasm between life and thought. Man not only knows, as is the case with some other animals, but he knows himself, i.e. man knows that he knows while the other animals, at best, can only know. Man is unique in the universe because he is a *person*, i.e. a center-of-consciousness, a reflective or intelligent being. Man, therefore, still holds a

---

[23]*The Phenomenon of Man*, p. 165.

[24]About thirty million years ago the Miocene apes or Dryopithecinae of Africa represented a heterogeneous genetic population from which the present chimpanzee, gorilla, and man have emerged.

[25]Teilhard's phenomenology is radically different from the nonhistorical analysis of consciousness developed in the writings of Edmund Husserl.

[26]We have noted that Teilhard referred to this as cephalization in general and cerebralization or cerebration in particular; a neural extension of complexity-consciousness.

special place in nature.[27] From *without* the human zoological group represents just one other biological species, but from *within* the human phylum represented, for Teilhard, the continuation of the spiritualization of the cosmos. Teilhard's philosophical anthropology is anthropocentric, for he saw planetary evolution as a preparation for the emergence of man, and held that its completion would be realized in the fulfillment of the human species.

B. CRITICAL THRESHOLDS IN THE EVOLUTIONARY LITERATURE

Wallace, Fiske, Bergson, Alexander, Smuts, and Morgan also held that there were qualitative leaps in evolution and therefore argued that man represents such a leap. As a result, they maintained that man differs in *kind* from the other lower or earlier animals. But Lamarck, Schopenhauer, Spencer, Darwin, Huxley, Nietzsche, Haeckel, Marx, Engels, Lenin, Sellars, and Dewey held that evolution represents a continuum without sudden leaps. They argued that man differs merely in *degree* from the other primates. The distinction between man differing in *kind* or *degree* from the other animals is crucial, as it determines whether man is believed to have a supernatural aspect or to be merely a natural product of biological evolution respectively.[28]

---

[27]Teilhard did not believe in the orthodox interpretation of Adam and Eve or Original Sin. Scientifically, it is possible but not very probable that the human phylum could have originated from just two individuals. One may safely assume that Teilhard believed the human species to have originated from a population of pre-humans in central Africa rather than a single couple as is recorded in *Genesis*. Likewise, he favored a monophyletic rather than a polyphyletic interpretation of human evolution, i.e. that man originated and developed in *one* general location before his global dispersion. Teilhard also held that the human soul was a natural product of evolution, although he will argue for its immortality; an inference from his assumption that the *radial* energy of man differs in *kind* from the *radial* energy of the other animals. And since for Teilhard there was no First Couple to start the human race, the doctrine of Original Sin takes on a cosmic dimension. It means that everything in the universe is imperfect proportional to its spatio-temporal distance from God. But through evolution, Teilhard held that the universe is perfecting itself. These positions were primarily responsible for his exile and silencing in 1926.

[28]The two positions are not always clear, e.g. although a naturalist, Smuts held that man represents a new *kind* of phenomenon in emergent evolution. But Smuts did not use this assumption as an argument for the immortality of the human soul.

Wallace held that there were distinct stages in evolution, i.e. the inorganic, organic, conscious, and spiritual levels, and that matter is ultimately will-force. Like Teilhard, his position held that Darwinism was necessary but not sufficient to account for biological evolution in general and human evolution in particular. He had rightly rejected Darwin's acceptance of Lamarckian "Use and Disuse" and "The Inheritance of Acquired Characteristics."[29] For Wallace, naturalism needed to be supplemented with a spiritualism.

Wallace held that man's mental abilities were superior to his needs for survival, and that a spiritualistic explanation was necessary for this discrepancy. He argued that man's mathematical, musical, artistic, and metaphysical faculties, as well as his speech, wit, humor, morality, naked and sensitive skin, and specialized and perfected brain, hands, and feet, could not have progressively developed in continuity by degree from animals as a result of natural selection or the survival of the fittest to survive and repro-

---

[29]It was embarrassing to Darwin that he could not scientifically account for the appearance of variations in biological organisms. As a result of his ignorance of population genetics and underestimation of the age of the earth, he reluctantly resorted to a Lamarckian theory of heredity, his doctrine of Pangenesis, to supplement his three methods of transformationism: (a) "natural selection" or "survival of the fittest" (referred to today as differential reproduction); (b) sexual selection; (c) artificial selection or domestication. Darwin's doctrine of Pangenesis held that each organ of an organism contributed a gemmule to the hereditary material. The modification of any organ would result in a corresponding modification of the gemmule within that organ, and such modifications were held by Darwin to appear in the offspring. The experiments of August Weismann at the close of the last century helped to discredit Lamarckian doctrines. See August Weismann: *The Evolutionary Theory*. London, Edward Arnold, 1904. Ironically Gregor Johann Mendel, an Austrian monk and contemporary of Darwin's, had been experimenting with the inheritance of garden peas. He published the basic laws of genetics in an unacknowledged manuscript in 1866. See Gregor Mendel: *Experiments in Plant Hybridisation*. Cambridge, Harvard University Press, 1967. The manuscript was discovered by Hugo DeVries and two other scientists simultaneously in 1900.

duce (differential reproduction) .[30] In a series of essays, Wallace presented his position:

> If the views I have here endeavoured to sustain have any foundation, they give us a new argument for placing man apart, as not only the head and culminating point of the grand series of organic nature, but as in some degree a new and distinct order of being. . . . The inference I would draw from this class of phenomena is, that a superior intelligence has guided the development of man in a definite direction, and for a special purpose, just as man guides the development of many animal and vegetable forms.[31]

And in a later work he wrote:

> . . . I fully accept Mr. Darwin's conclusion as to the essential identity of man's bodily structure with that of the higher mammalia, and his descent from some ancestral form common to man and the anthropoid apes. . . . We find the most pronounced distinction between man and the anthropoid apes in the size and complexity of his brain. . . . Because man's physical structure has been developed from an animal form by natural selection, it does not necessarily follow that his mental nature, even though developed *pari passu* with it, has been developed by the same causes only. . . . It could not have been developed by variation and natural selection alone. . . . The special faculties we have been discussing clearly point to the existence in man of something which he has not derived from his animal progenitors—something which we may best refer to as being of a spiritual essence or nature, capable of progressive development under favourable conditions.[32]

Like Teilhard, he claimed that man's mental structure separated him from the rest of the biological kingdom. Fiske was of the

---

[30]Herbert Spencer originated the concept of "the survival of the fittest." In *The Origin of Species*, Darwin admitted that his expression was more accurate and sometimes equally convenient than his own principle of "natural selection." Unfortunately Spencer and others were to overextend the doctrine by adopting it as a social principle. For the impact of Darwinism on theories of society, see Richard Hofstadter: *Social Darwinism in American Thought*. Boston, Beacon, 1955.

[31]Wallace: *Contributions to the Theory of Natural Selection*, pp. 324, 359.

[32]Wallace: *Darwinism*, pp. 461, 457, 463, 474. The position held by Wallace mirrors the late position adopted by Fiske, i.e. Wallace held that there was an unseen universe of Spirit to which the world of matter is altogether subordinate. In short, for Wallace the universe *is* the WILL of higher intelligences or of one Supreme Intelligence.

same opinion. In his *Outlines of Cosmic Philosophy* (1874) he acknowledged the structural differences between man's brain and those of the great apes. His original position was naturalistic:

> By a continuous differential compounding of impressions, we pass, through infinitesimal stages, from the relatively homogeneous and simple set of correspondences known as reflex action, manifested alike by the highest and the lowest animals, to those exceedingly complex and heterogeneous sets of correspondences known as reason and volition, which are manifested only by the highest animals, and in their greatest complexity by man alone.[33]

In his later works, Fiske took a spiritualistic orientation. (There had been a slow break from the Spencerian philosophy to a theistic interpretation of the universe.) In *The Destiny of Man* (1884), Fiske's change of attitude is obvious:

> Through the complication of effects the heaping up of minute differences in degree has ended in bringing forth a difference in *kind*. . . . For my own part, therefore, I believe in the immortality of the soul, not in the sense in which I accept the demonstrable truths of science, but as a supreme act of faith in the reasonableness of God's work.[34]

In *Through Nature to God* (1899), Fiske presented his final position.

> . . . we have at last in man a creature different in kind from his predecessors. . . . The moment we consider the minds of man and ape, the gap between the two is immeasurable. . . . Nay, you must even dichotomize the universe, putting Man on one side and all things else on the other.[35]

The writings of Wallace and Fiske represent early reactions to

---

[33]Fiske: *Outlines of Cosmic Philosophy*, vol. 3, P. 238. In the same volume see pp. 194-240 for a naturalistic interpretation of the evolution of mind. It is interesting to note that Fiske had overextended into the religious realm Darwin's concern for adaptation. He held that established religions were means of human adaptation to the Unknowable.

[34]John Fiske: *The Destiny of Man Viewed in the Light of His Origin*. Boston, Houghton, Mifflin, 1897, pp. 56, 116.

[35]John Fiske: *Through Nature to God*. Boston, Houghton, Mifflin, 1899, pp. 53, 82.

the mechanical and agnostic positions advocated by Darwin[36] and Huxley. They had sought to reconcile the theory of evolution and the established teachings of Christianity by replacing materialism with spiritualism and by maintaining that man represents a higher ontological position above the biological realm and not merely the continuation of that realm. This position allowed for the assumption that man's soul is free and immortal.

By the close of the nineteenth century the geological and paleontological evidence to support evolution was conclusive. Likewise, the rediscovery of the Mendelian principles of genetics eliminated any need to resort to vitalism or finalism as an explanation to account for the emergence of novelty.[37] In light of this increase in scientific evidence, the spiritualistic assumptions of Wallace and Fiske became unwarranted. A naturalistic conception of man was replacing the dualistic interpretation that had dominated European thought for nearly two thousand years. Yet it is not surprising that attempts were still made to preserve the traditional conception of man in spite of the success of the sciences. Such a restoration required a subjective methodology to supplement scientific inquiry.

Bergson held that reason was incapable of grasping the essence of nature, i.e. the fluidity of time. Mathematics merely spatialized reality, but intuition revealed the internal flow of consciousness as well as the external flow of evolution. As a result of his subjective methodology, he had dichotomized the universe ontologically between matter and spirit. He recognized the vegetative, instinctive, and rational forms of life as three divergent directions of creative evolution, the difference between them being one of *kind.* As a result, man represented the pinnacle of conscious development:

> . . . among conscious beings themselves, man comes to occupy a privileged place. Between him and the animals the difference is no longer

---

[36]Despite the implications of his theory of evolution, Darwin remained agnostic; he did not wish to associate himself with atheism, and disappointed Karl Marx when he did not accept the dedication of the second edition of *Das Kapital* (1882).

[37]See L. C. Dunn: *A Short History of Genetics; The Development of Some of the Main Lines of Thought: 1864-1939.* New York, McGraw-Hill, 1965.

one of degree, but of kind. . . . So that, in the last analysis, man might be considered the reason for the existence of the entire organization of life on our planet.[38]

This view of man misrepresents his true nature. An ontological dualism which separates self-consciousness from consciousness distorts the unity and continuity of the universe in general, and the unity and continuity of man with the evolution of nature in particular. Bergson has made a false assumption when he maintains that the human mind and its body are merely "united" through the activity of perception:

> Not only does the hypothesis of an equivalence between the psychical state and the cerebral state imply a downright absurdity, . . . but the facts, examined without prejudice, certainly seem to indicate that the relation of the psychical to the physical is just that of the machine to the screw.[39]

While the activity of consciousness and the physical brain are not equivalent, it does not follow that consciousness and the brain are unrelated. Only a distinction is needed, not a separation. Mental activity requires the proper functioning of the brain and cannot exist without it. Just as seeing and hearing require the proper functioning of the eyes and ears respectively, so does rational activity require a brain. In short, without a brain self-consciousness would be unthinkable. Bergson's position ignores this basic fact. Likewise, it deprecates the continuity of conscious activity manifested in biological evolution when it places man outside the animal kingdom. Only from an unwarranted anthropocentric orientation can it be claimed that "man is the 'term' and the 'end' of evolution."[40] Each animal and plant has specialized in its structure and behavior in order to adapt successfully to its particular environment. Man's specialized brain has allowed him to adapt very successfully to a variety of environments. But the human brain is the product of chance variations in genetic makeup as well as adaptive and survival pressures operating on the organism. Had Bergson adopted an ontological monism while

---

[38]Bergson: *Creative Evolution*, pp. 200, 203.
[39]*Ibid.*, p. 386.
[40]*Ibid.*, p. 289.

merely distinguishing between mental activity in its various modes and its biological grounding in the nervous system and brain, his view of man would have been in step with the advancement of the natural sciences.

As an emergent evolutionist, Alexander had seen the cosmos as a hierarchy of qualities differing in *kind*. He distinguished between the emergent quality of mind in general and the various levels of minds each differing in kind or quality but not in degree.[41] Like Alexander, the emergent evolutionists were significant in emphasizing that mental functions succeeded but are dependent upon biological structures, just as living functions succeeded but are dependent upon biological structures. But it must be remembered that the emergence of all new structures and functions occurs within a space-time continuum. As a result, there are no sudden "leaps" or "gaps" in cosmic evolution to justify maintaining the emergence of new ontological spheres or levels of being. All known manifestations of evolutionary phenomena are ontologically reducible to matter and/or energy. Since matter and energy are merely two manifestations of the same basic stuff of the universe, scientific evidence supports an ontological monism.

Smuts held that the quality of Mind represented a new product of emergent evolution:

> The appearance of Mind, therefore, especially at the human level where it is most marked, seems to constitute a break in the even and regular advance of Evolution, and to mark a new departure of a very far-reaching character. . . . The super-structure of Mind is immeasurably greater than the brain or neural structure on which it rests, and is something of a quite different order, which marks a revolutionary departure from organic order whence it originated. . . . Mind is a new type of structure of the immaterial or spiritual kind, and so also is its field.[42]

One might suspect that by maintaining Mind to be a radically new kind of structure, Smuts was arguing for a dualistic conception of man. Yet this was not the case, for he viewed man as a wholistic structure in keeping with his philosophy of Holism:

---

[41]Alexander: *Space, Time, and Deity,* vol. 2, p. 69.
[42]Smuts: *Holism and Evolution,* pp. 233, 253.

Subtract mind, and the residue of body must shrink and shrivel into an unimaginable scrap-heap of organic activities. Similarly it is impossible to conceive mind as abstracted from the body. The disembodied soul is just as impossible a concept as the disminded body.[43]

C. EVOLUTION AS A CONTINUUM

Not all of the evolutionists held to the doctrine of critical thresholds. There were those naturalists who maintained the continuity of planetary evolution, i.e. that inorganic evolution passes into organic evolution, and organic evolution passes into psychosocial evolution without sudden interruptions. From this perspective human evolution is merely the continuation of mammalian evolution in general and primate evolution in particular. The emergence of man does not represent a radical departure from a materialistic interpretation of nature.

Lamarck was aware that nomenclature in natural history is a human construction that artificially categorizes the real continuity of biological evolution. Although his philosophy of zoology was vitalistic, teleological, and anthropocentric, it has merit in that it supported the continuity of nature and held that man differs from the other animals merely in his degree of complexity and the resulting faculties:

If the procedure of nature is attentively examined, it will be seen that in the creating or giving existence to her productions, she has never acted suddenly or by a single leap, but has always worked by degrees towards a gradual and imperceptible development: consequently all her products and transformations are everywhere clearly subject to this law of progress.

If we follow the operations of nature, we shall see that she created by successive stages all the tissues and organs of animals, that she gradually brought them to completion and perfection, and that in the same way by slow degrees she modified, animalised, and compounded all the internal fluids of the animals she had brought into existence; so that in course of time they were brought to the condition in which we now see them.[44]

As a result of his position, Lamarck held that man is distinct

---

[43]*Ibid.*, p. 268.
[44]Lamarck: *Zoological Philosophy*, pp. 304-305.

from other animals because of his mental faculties, i.e. man's acquired "supreme superiority" is due to his reasoning faculty which differs only in degree from the monkeys and apes.[45] But the evolutionary position in *Zoological Philosophy* (1809) was highly speculative, for Lamarck lacked the scientific evidence needed to support his hypotheses. In philosophy there emerged a concern for planetary and/or cosmic development. Hegel's *The Phenomenology of Spirit* (1807) emphasized the dialectical process in social and mental development, but was nonevolutionary. Hegel, like Aristotle, had held to the fixity of species. (Unfortunately, Plato's eternal and unchanging Forms were still present in the philosophical literature.)

The evolutionary theory was anticipated in the works of Arthur Schopenhauer. Unlike Kant, he held that the noumenal realm was knowable; ultimate reality is a universal Will of which all phenomena are the temporary manifestations. In his major work, *The World as Will and Representation* (1818), Schopenhauer clearly held to the unity of the universal Will as well as maintaining that its objectifications form a natural hierarchy. Although his position is anthropocentric, the evolutionary perspective is evident:

> In order to appear in its proper significance, the Idea of man would need to manifest itself, not alone and torn apart, but accompanied by all the grades downwards through all the forms of animals, through the plant kingdom to the inorganic. They all supplement one another for the complete objectification of the will. They are as much presupposed by the Idea of man as the blossoms of the tree presuppose its leaves, branches, trunk, and root. They form a pyramid, of which the highest point is man. . . . By virtue of such necessity, man needs the animals for his support, the animals in their grades need one another, and also the plants, which again need soil, water, chemical elements and their combinations, the planet, the sun, rotation and motion round the sun, the obliquity of the ecliptic, and so on.[46]

---

[45]*Ibid.*, pp. 169-173.

[46]Arthur Schopenhauer: *The World as Will and Representation.* New York, Dover, 1966, vol. 1, pp. 153, 154. Schopenhauer's philosophy retained a Platonic influence, for Ideas mediate between the cosmic Will and its objectifications. Like Schopenhauer, Alexander, Sellars, Morgan, and Teilhard represented the structure of evolution as a pyramid with man as its peak.

For Schopenhauer, the visible products of the development of the cosmic Will differ only in degree, forming a hierarchy of slight gradations. Since man is a product of nature and entirely within nature, it necessarily follows that he differs from the other animals only in degree:

> Nothing leads more definitely to a recognition of the identity of the essential nature in animal and human phenomena than a study of zoology and anatomy. . . . One must be really quite blind or totally chloroformed by the *foetor Judaicus* not to recognize that the essential and principal thing in the animal and man is the same, and that what distinguishes the one from the other is not to be found in the primary and original principle, in the archaeus, in the inner nature, in the kernel of the two phenomena, such kernel being in both alike the *will* of the individual; but only in the secondary, in the intellect, in the degree of the cognitive faculty. In man this degree is incomparably higher through the addition of the faculty of *abstract* knowledge, called *reason*. Yet this superiority is traceable only to a greater cerebral development, and hence to the somatic difference of a single part, the brain, and in particular, its quantity. On the other hand, the similarity between animal and man is incomparably greater, both psychically and somatically.[47]

Schopenhauer reacted against Kant's nonempirical and theological orientation, for he held that philosophy should begin with natural experience. And even though he gave a privileged position to will, his naturalistic tendency in placing man entirely within nature was a welcomed change from the followers of Cartesian dualism.

The first comprehensive philosophy of evolution was represented in the "Synthetic Philosophy" of Herbert Spencer.[48] In *First Principles* (1862), he advocated the general law of transformation and equivalence for vital and mental forces:

> Various classes of facts thus unite to prove that the law of metamorphosis, which holds among the physical forces, holds equally between them and the mental forces.[49]

---

[47] Arthur Schopenhauer: *On the Basis of Morality.* New York, Bobbs-Merrill, 1965, pp. 177-178. By *"foetor Judaicus"* Schopenhauer means "Judaic odor."

[48] In *Zoological Philosophy*, Lamarck had separated the mineral, vegetative, and animal kingdoms, as well as holding to the spontaneous generation of simple plants and animals.

[49] Spencer: *First Principles*, p. 223.

For Spencer, mental forces were the result of vital forces, just as vital forces were the result of physico-chemical forces. In fact, the whole cosmos was the manifestation of Force. His monistic position left no room for maintaining a dualistic conception of man.

For the first half of the nineteenth century, inquiries into man's proper place in nature lacked scientific evidence for geology, paleontology, and biology were still underdeveloped sciences in contrast to astronomy and physics. Thomas Henry Huxley, who had defended Darwinism against the attacks of the Church, was the first to write a book for the sole purpose of scientifically substantiating the application of biological evolution to the phyletic development of man. In *Evidence as to Man's Place in Nature* (1863), Huxley referred to established knowledge in comparative anatomy and embryology, primatology, and human paleontology. Where Darwin had held the "mystery of mysteries" to be the *origin* of species, Huxley held that the "question of questions" was the *origin* of man. In his first work, Huxley established his "Pithecometra Thesis:"

> Thus, whatever systems of organs be studied, the comparison of their modifications in the ape series leads to one and the same result— that the structural differences which separate Man from the Gorilla and the Chimpanzee are not so great as those which separate the Gorilla from the lower apes.[50]

As a direct result of this thesis, he placed man totally within nature:

> I have endeavoured to show that no absolute structural line of demarcation, wider than that between the animals which immediately succeed us in the scale, can be drawn between the animal world and ourselves; and I may add the expression of my belief that the attempt to draw a physical distinction is equally futile, and that even the highest faculties of feeling and of intellect begin to germinate in lower forms of life.[51]

---

[50]Thomas H. Huxley: *Man's Place in Nature.* Ann Arbor, The University of Michigan Press, 1959, p. 123. In general, Huxley held that the physical and psychical differences were greater between the monkeys and apes than they were between the apes and man.

[51]*Ibid.*, p. 129.

In *On the Origin of Species* (1863), he repeated his position:

> . . . I have strongly maintained on sundry occasions that if Mr. Darwin's views are sound, they apply as much to man as to the lower mammals, seeing that it is perfectly demonstrable that the structural differences which separate man from the apes are not greater than those which separate some apes from others. There cannot be the slightest doubt in the world that the argument which applies to the improvement of the horse from an earlier stock, or of ape from ape, applies to the improvement of man from some simpler and lower stock than man. There is not a single faculty— functional or structural, moral, intellectual, or instinctive,—there is no faculty whatever that is not capable of improvement; there is no faculty whatsoever which does not depend upon structure, and as structure tends to vary, it is capable of being improved.[52]

Huxley's brave move had anticipated the future work of Darwin.[53] When the latter had published *The Origin of Species* (1859), giving scientific evidence to support his theory of evolution, the unfavorable reactions from the Church and some academicians were so strong that he withheld from extending his theory to also account for the biological origin and development of man. In fact, Darwin had even been forced into an early publi-

---

[52]Thomas H. Huxley: *On the Origin of Species or, the Causes of the Phenomena of Organic Nature*. Ann Arbor, The University of Michigan Press, 1968, p. 140. For other relevant works see Huxley's *Darwiniana: Essays* (1893) and *Discourses: Biological and Geological* (1894). For a second work touching on the extension of evolution to include the human phylum see Sir Charles Lyell's *The Geological Evidences of the Antiquity of Man* (1863), chap. 24. Lyell had advocated geological evolution to replace the theory of catastrophism advocated by Georges Cuvier. Ironically, Lyell himself never accepted human evolution but held to special creations in the biological realm. (In 1867, Lyell's Darwinism was ambiguous.)

[53]For pre-Darwinian thought on the "Great Chain of Being" and evolutionary thought, see Bentley Glass, Owsei Temkin, and William L. Straus, Jr. (Eds.): *Forerunners of Darwin: 1745-1895*. Baltimore, The Johns Hopkins Press, 1968, and Arthur O. Lovejoy: *The Great Chain of Being: A Study of the History of an Idea*. New York, Harper and Row, 1965. For some reactions to Darwinism, see Philip P. Wiener: *Evolution and the Founders of Pragmatism*. New York, Harper and Row, 1965.

cation of *The Origin of Species* (1859).[54] In this work, the ever cautious Darwin had merely remarked that, "Much light will be thrown on the origin of man and his history."[55] But twelve years later Darwin finally did extend his evolutionary perspective to

---

[54]Darwin had studied medicine and theology, but preferred natural history, notably entomology, marine biology, and geology. At the suggestion of the botanist John S. Henslow, Darwin accepted the position of naturalist aboard the H.M.S. Beagle under Captain Robert FitzRoy; this was the result of the encouragement of Darwin's uncle who was successful in persuading Darwin's own father that the idea was worthwhile. Darwin was only 22, and believed in the account of Creation as recorded in *Genesis*. For five years the Beagle circumnavigated the world, and Darwin collected the scientific evidence needed to support his theory of "descent with modification." Three events were primarily responsible for his formulation of the theory of evolution: (a) Darwin was greatly influenced by Lyell's theory of uniformitarianism as presented in his *Principles of Geology* (1830), for it advocated geological evolution; (b) the Galápagos Archipelago gave him the opportunity to study the adaptive relationships between animals and plants and their environments, particularly the finches which represented an excellent example of "speeded-up" microevolution—the relationship between their beak size and shape and their diet would later give Darwin the needed evidence to support his theory of natural selection; (c) his reading of Thomas Robert Malthus' "An Essay of the Principle of Population as it Affects the Future Improvement of Society with Remarks on the Speculations of Mr. Godwin, M. Condorcet, and other Writers" (1798) gave him the concept of the survival of the fittest. He wrote a brief outline of his theory of evolution in 1844. While living in isolation at Kent, England, Darwin received a manuscript from Alfred Russel Wallace who was doing research in the Malay Archipelago. The essay was entitled, "On the Tendency of Varieties to Depart Indefinitely from the Original Type" (1858). Darwin and Wallace had both simultaneously expounded natural selection as the primary method of biological evolution. On July 1, 1858, both Darwin and Wallace were read before the Linnaean Society of England, their papers entitled collectively, "On the Tendency of Species to form Varieties; and on the Perpetuation of Varieties and Species by Natural Means of Selection"; the papers were published in the *Journal of the Proceedings of the Linnaean Society*. Credit for the theory of evolution was given to Darwin because of his overwhelming evidence. It is unfortunate that Darwin's success has overshadowed Wallace's contributions to evolutionary literature. Darwin published his "premature" work the following year (1859). For recent literature on Darwin, see Philip Appleman (Ed.): *Darwin*. New York, Norton, 1970; Gertrude Himmelfarb: *Darwin and the Darwinian Revolution*. New York, Norton, 1968; and Alan Moorehead: *Darwin and the Beagle*. New York, Harper and Row, 1970.

[55]Charles Darwin: *The Origin of Species and The Descent of Man*. New York, The Modern Library, 1936, p. 373. The addition of the adjective "much" in the second edition of the work shows that Darwin's confidence was growing. His work had caused such a stir in intellectual circles that he refrained from including man within the evolutionary theory until there was conclusive evidence.

include a naturalistic interpretation of the development of the human species. *The Descent of Man* (1871) supplemented Huxley's work by adding evidence from homologous and rudimentary structures. Darwin argued for the principle of gradual evolution, held that man differs merely in degree from the other primates, and rightly prophesied that man originated from an ape-like population in Africa. His naturalistic position concerning man's place in nature is explicit:

> . . . there is no fundamental difference between man and the higher mammals in their mental faculties. . . . There can be no doubt that the differences between the mind of the lowest man and that of the highest animal is immense. . . . Nevertheless the difference in mind between man and the higher animals, great as it is, certainly is one of degree and not of kind.[56]

The works of Huxley and Darwin had given scientific support to the evolutionary hypothesis conceived by Lamarck, i.e. that existing forms have emerged from pre-existing forms. Yet the method of natural selection, even if supplemented by sexual selection and domestication, could not account for the *origin* of variations. Knowledge of genetics and an understanding of mutations were not forthcoming until the twentieth century.[57] Mendel's isolated research was the only exception.

Ernst Haeckel, referred to as "Germany's Darwin," defended

---

[56]*Ibid.*, pp. 446, 494. Also see pp. 456-457, 462, 496, 513, 541, 557-558, 911-912. For references to human evolution, see pp. 512-528, 541, 562, 872, 895, 909, 911, 920.

[57]Darwinism lacked an understanding of heredity. The modern theory of evolution or neo-Darwinism is referred to as the "Synthetic Theory of Evolution" for it supplements the Darwinian principles with population genetics; there is no longer any need to rely upon the Lamarckian doctrines as the Russians had erroneously done under the direction of Trofim Lysenko in the 1930's and 1940's. Modern genetics disproves the inheritance of acquired characters; the distinction between somatic cells and gametes or sex cells is crucial. Natural selection is referred to as differential reproduction to denote that the survival of individuals also means that these individuals have survived and therefore are capable of producing further offspring to continue the genetic population. For an account of the "Synthetic Theory of Evolution," see Theodosius Dobzhansky: *Genetics and the Origin of Species.* New York, Columbia University Press, 1964. Teilhard held that even neo-Darwinism, with its concern for genetic and environmental influences, was not sufficient to account for the orthogenetic character of planetary evolution.

the Darwinian theory of evolution and concerned himself with the philosophical implications of the theory.[58] In an early work his naturalistic attitude is already explicit:

> I personally consider the descent of man from the apes as equally certain; nay, I regard this most important and pregnant genealogical hypothesis as one of those which, up to the present time, rest on the best empirical basis. . . . The problem of the origin and nature of consciousness is only a special case of the general problem of the connection of matter and force.[59]

We have already seen that Haeckel advocated an ontological monism. Now to account for the emergence of consciousness within an evolutionary perspective, he adopted a panpsychic position[60] but rejected the *anthropolatrous* doctrine by maintaining that the human mind differs from the psychic activity of lower animals merely in degree. His position was in agreement with those of Huxley and Darwin:

> Comparative psychology teaches us to recognise a very long series of successive steps in the development of soul in the animal kingdom. . . . Our human body has been built up slowly and by degrees from a long series of vertebrate ancestors, and this is also true of our soul; as a function of our brain it has gradually been developed in reciprocal action and reaction with this its bodily organ. . . . The conception of a personal immortality cannot be maintained. . . . We can as little think of our individual soul as separate from our brain, as we can conceive the voluntary motion of our arm apart

---

[58]For Haeckel's scientific treatment of human evolution, emphasizing embryology and phylogeny, see Ernst Haeckel: *The Evolution of Man: A Popular Scientific Study.* New York, G. P. Putnam's Sons, 1910.

[59]Ernst Haeckel: *Freedom in Science and Teaching.* London, C. Kegan Paul, 1879, pp. 41, 102.

[60]Haeckel's position of panpsychism resulted from the investigations of comparative psychology. A distinction, however, should be made between a "weak" and a "strong" form of panpsychism. A "weak" form of panpsychism merely maintains that all living objects manifest an aspect, and therefore a degree, of psychic development or sensitivity; this is Haeckel's position. However, a "strong" form of panpsychism advocates that ultimately everything in reality is psychic in nature and therefore an ontological position of objective idealism is necessary; this is Teilhard's argument. A naturalist may support ontological monism, i.e. materialism, for the degree of sensitivity manifested by a biological organism depends upon the development of the nervous system; one may, therefore, speak of the materialistic emergence of psychic activity.

from the contraction of its muscles, or the circulation of our blood apart from the action of the heart.[61]

Unlike Huxley and Darwin, Haeckel was not reticent in expounding the naturalistic implications of the theory of evolution. His philosophy of man was grounded in the natural sciences. Unlike Teilhard, he held that the evolution of man could be sufficiently accounted for by the sciences, i.e. there was no need to ignore or distort established natural facts by dogmatically holding to unverifiable philosophical assumptions for the sake of retaining a theological orientation. He was bold enough to clearly point out that there was no longer any legitimate grounds for believing in a supernatural nature of man. In short, there was no need to construct elaborate philosophical systems in an attempt to reconcile the special sciences with theology. Theology was simply being replaced by scientific understanding.

Leibniz, Kant, and Hegel had favored subjectivism. In *The Riddle of the Universe* (1900), Haeckel presented his naturalistic philosophy of man and the universe. He had the advantage of an evolutionary perspective supported by astronomy, paleontology, biology,[62] anthropology, and psychology. He focused his attention on the nature of man, and as a zoologist and philosopher held to the natural evolution of the rational "soul:"

> What we call the soul is, in my opinion, a natural phenomenon. . . . The striking resemblance of man's psychic activity to that of the higher animals—especially our nearest relatives among the mammals —is a familiar fact. . . . Man has no single mental faculty which is his exclusive prerogative. His whole psychic life differs from that of the nearest related mammals only in degree, and not in kind; quantitatively, not qualitatively. . . . If we ascribe "personal immortality" to man, we are bound to grant it also to the higher animals. . . . If we take a comprehensive glance at all that modern anthro-

---

[61]Ernst Haeckel: *Monism as Connecting Religion and Science*. London, Adam and Charles Black, 1895, pp. 8, 40, 51-52, 57.

[62]Haeckel himself contributed to the understanding of embryology and its relationship to phylogeny. He formulated the "Biogenetic Law" which held that, "*Ontogenesis is a brief and rapid recapitulation of phylogenesis,* determined by the physiological functions of heredity (generation) and adaptation (maintenance)." The concept is true in a *very general* way. See Haeckel, *The Riddle of the Universe*, p. 81.

pology, psychology, and cosmology teach with regard to athanatism, we are forced to this definite conclusion: "The belief in the immortality of the human soul is a dogma which is in hopeless contradiction with the most solid empirical truths of modern science."[63]

Haeckel acknowledged that reason does distinguish man from the lower animals, but reason is not a transcendental aspect of the human mind. He held that reason is an activity of the human mind which has evolved along with the evolution of the brain:

> Pure reason, the highest quality of civilized man, was gradually evolved from the intelligence of the savage, and this in turn from the instincts of the apes and lower mammals.[64]

In his last work, Haeckel retained his naturalism, rejecting Cartesian dualism in favor of an evolutionary monism:

> A long series of intermediate stages connects the psychic life of the higher animals with that of man on the one side, and that of the lower animals on the other. There was no such thing as a sharp dividing line, as Descartes supposed. . . . The human soul has only reached its present height by a long period of gradual evolution; it differs in degree, not in kind, from the soul of the higher mammals; and thus it cannot in any case be immortal.[65]

Like Haeckel, Nietzsche adopted a naturalistic position that rejected the Christian belief in personal immortality:

> But the awakened and knowing say: body am I entirely, and nothing else; and soul is only a word for something about the body. . . . The soul is as mortal as the body. . . . The great lie of personal immortality destroys all reason, everything natural in the instincts. . . . "Immortality" conceded to every Peter and Paul has so far been the greatest, the most malignant, attempt to assassinate *noble* humanity.[66]

---

[63]Haeckel: *The Riddle of the Universe*, pp. 89, 98, 107, 201, 210. Continued research in primatology substantiates Haeckel's position.

[64]Ernst Haeckel: *The Wonders of Life: A Popular Study of Biological Philosophy*. New York, Harper and Brothers, 1905, p. 470. Haeckel's position is a reaction against the theologically oriented position of Kant, who was not an evolutionist.

[65]Haeckel: *Last Words on Evolution*, pp. 124, 145.

[66]Nietzsche: *The Portable Nietzsche*, pp. 146, 333, 618, 619.

... this belief ought to be expelled from science![67]

Marx, Engels, and Lenin had also adopted naturalistic positions. Marx reacted against Hegel's objective idealism by establishing a materialistic position; the universe was not the eternal, dialectical unfolding of Spirit toward unity and freedom, i.e. Absolute Knowledge or Philosophy, but the dialectical struggle of matter in motion. He went further than Ludwig Feuerbach, for he not only negated theology but held that no conception of God was necessary to understand man's place in nature (Feuerbach had only reduced Theology to Anthropology, claiming "God" to be the social relationships between men). For Marx, theology alienated man from his true *natural* origin. Man cannot be abstracted from his historicosocial context:

> To say that man *lives* from nature means that nature is his *body* with which he must remain in a continuous interchange in order not to die. The statement that the physical and mental life of man, and nature, are interdependent means simply that nature is interdependent with itself, for man is a part of nature. . . . Conscious life activity distinguishes man from the life activity of animals. . . . Activity and mind are social in their content as well as in their *origin;* they are *social* activity and *social* mind.[68]

Engels had also adopted an evolutionary perspective that was grounded in dialectical materialism:

> All chemical processes reduce themselves to processes of chemical attraction and repulsion. Finally, in organic life the formation of the cell nucleus is likewise to be regarded as a polarisation of the living protein material, and from the simple cell onwards, the theory of evolution demonstrates how each advances up to the most compli-

---

[67]Friedrich Nietzsche: *Beyond Good and Evil: Prelude to a Philosophy of the Future.* New York, Vintage Books, 1966, p. 20. Nietzsche's doctrine of Eternal Recurrence did not advocate a Christian form of personal immortality; it was grounded in materialism and determinism. It merely argued for the eternal return of persons within the successive, finite, identical cycles of cosmic evolution. Although he held that God was dead as a meaningful concept for there was no metaphysical correlate for the belief, Nietzsche could not accept the finitude of human existence. His doctrine of Eternal Recurrence could be interpreted as a compromise between Christianity and fatalism.

[68]Fromm: *Marx's Concept of Man,* pp. 101, 129.

cated plant on the one side, and up to man on the other, is effected by the continual conflict between heredity and adaptation.[69]

Like Teilhard, Engels was aware that vertebrate evolution manifests a continued increase in the complexity of the nervous system, resulting in greater degrees of consciousness:

> Vertebrates.—Their essential character: the *grouping of the whole body about the nervous system.* Thereby the development to self-consciousness, etc., becomes possible.[70]

Like Marx and Engels, Lenin had also advocated dialectical materialism. The implications of his position were the same—man is totally within nature, since he is a material product of natural development. Therefore, self-consciousness is dependent upon a material organ, the human brain:

> . . . consciousness without matter does not exist, and apparently not even without a nervous system! That is, consciousness and sensation are secondary.[71]

The historicosocial, dialectical materialism advocated by Marx, Engels, and Lenin held to the continuity of nature. Biological evolution continued into psychosocial evolution; social change provided the possibility for the qualitative, collective improvement of the human condition. There was no need to reconcile established facts with theological assumptions. Teilhard shared their concern for progress and the unity of a collective mankind, but always from a spiritualistic orientation.

As an emergent evolutionist, Sellars held that new properties emerge as a result of the evolution of matter into new organizations. As a result of his critical realism, he maintained a naturalistic or bio-psychological view of the mind-body "problem."

> The *whole* of man must be included in nature, and nature so conceived that his inclusion is possible. . . . Thought is retrospective

---

[69]Engels: *Dialectics of Nature*, p. 207. Teilhard had favored the influence of mind on the direction of evolution, i.e. vitalism, over the influences of heredity and adaptation.

[70]*Ibid.*, p. 201.

[71]Lenin: *Materialism and Empirio-Criticism*, p. 88.

and supervenes upon reality. . . . Assuredly, man is a part of nature, but his differences from inorganic nature must not be overlooked.[72]

For Sellars, man has emerged out of organic evolution, and mind has emerged by *degree* as a new property or category of highly complex organization. Unlike Teilhard, no new ontological position is held by the emergence of human consciousness. He held that all emergent properties are grounded in matter:

> . . . consciousness is not a new stuff in any metaphysical sense. . . . The mind is the brain as known in its functioning. . . . We conceive mind as an activity and believe that it is to be assigned to the complex neural process which mediates behavior. . . . The brain-mind is an organ whose function is the adjustment of the individual.[73]

He held that consciousness is an activity totally dependent on the proper functioning of the brain. Therefore, human immortality is impossible since there cannot be personal consciousness without a brain:

> . . . the psychical is literally in the brain as a quality. . . . The ontological status of consciousness . . . is the qualitative dimension of a brain-event. It is the patterned brain-event as sentient.[74]

John Dewey[75] had also been greatly influenced by Charles Darwin.[76] As a naturalist he ruled out any theological assumptions, and saw nature as a continuum:

> The idea of development applied to nature involves differences of forms and qualities as surely as it rules out absolute breaches of continuity.[77]

---

[72]Sellars: *Evolutionary Naturalism*, pp. 20, 115, 259.

[73]*Ibid.*, pp. 283, 300, 308, 340.

[74]Roy Wood Sellars: *The Philosophy of Physical Realism.* New York, Russell and Russell, 1966, pp. 411, 414.

[75]It is interesting to note that three philosophers influenced by evolution, John Dewey, Henri Bergson, and Samuel Alexander, were born in 1859, the year of the publication of Charles Darwin's *The Origin of Species.*

[76]See John Dewey: *The Influence of Darwin on Philosophy.* Bloomington, Indiana University Press, 1965, pp. 1-19.

[77]John Dewey: *On Experience, Nature, and Freedom.* New York, Bobbs-Merrill, 1960, p. 236.

As a result of his naturalistic position, he rejected a dualistic interpretation of nature:

> That to which both mind and matter belong is the complex of events that constitute nature. . . . The objection to dualism is not just that it is a dualism, but that it forces upon us antithetical, non-convertible principles of formulation and interpretation. . . . The distinction between physical, psycho-physical, and mental is thus one of levels of increasing complexity and interaction among natural events. . . . Psycho-physical phenomena and higher mental phenomena may be admitted in their full empirical reality, without recourse to dualistic breach in historic, existential continuity.[78]

Thus human consciousness is not a simple, immortal substance but an activity or event which is temporal and grounded in matter:

> To see the organism *in* nature, the nervous system in the organism, the brain in the nervous system, the cortex in the brain is the answer to the problems which haunt philosophy. And when thus seen they will be seen to be *in*, not as marbles are in a box but as events are in history, in a moving, growing never finished process. . . . We cannot separate organic life and mind from physical nature without also separating nature from life and mind.[79]

Although Dewey recognized three major levels of development, (a) physico-chemical, (b) psycho-physical, and (c) human experience, he taught the continuity of nature.

D. FINAL INTERPRETATION

Why didn't Teilhard maintain the continuity of nature, i.e. the continuity of planetary evolution? We have already seen that his ontological monism and Law of increasing centro-Complexity-Consciousness were theologically grounded (cosmogenesis is the

---

[78]John Dewey: *Experience and Nature*. New York, Dover, 1958, pp. 75, 241, 261, 265-266.

[79]*Ibid.*, pp. 295, 296. Dewey's pragmatic philosophy, entitled "instrumentalism," "operationalism," "experimentalism," "functionalism," or "empirical naturalism," was greatly influenced by Darwin's concept of "natural selection." He held that ideas are instruments or tools to solve "problematic situations," that is to say that they allow for human adaptation and therefore survival. Although Dewey speaks of reality as events, he rejects all forms of Idealism.

directed spiritualization of the universe). Likewise, Teilhard's doctrine of critical thresholds is also theologically oriented but this only becomes apparent when we see its consequences in his view of man. He argued that since man represents a qualitative leap in biological evolution, he therefore represents a difference in *kind,* not merely in *degree,* from the other animals. As a direct result, man's mind, i.e. *radial* energy, is held to differ in *kind* from the *degrees* of *radial* energy manifested within the ascending hierarchy of biological complexification. What is the significance of this radical change of state in the evolution of *radial* energy? The answer is a theological assumption—personal immortality of the human soul.

Teilhard held that each species in the animal kingdom manifests its own particular *degree* of *radial* energy as a direct result of its *degree* of centro-complexification; the more advanced a species is in its complexification, the higher its position in the hierarchy of nature and the greater its *degree* of consciousness. At the death of an animal its *radial* energy is transformed into *tangential* energy. However, Teilhard argues that this is not the case at the death of a human being. Since human life resulted from the crossing of a critical threshold, human *radial* energy is unique from the psychic energies manifested by all other animals in the biosphere. Human *radial* energy does not change its nature as a result of the physical transformation of the human body at death, but continues to endure as a center-of-consciousness:

> Once formed, a reflective centre can no longer change except by involution upon itself. To outward appearance, admittedly, man disintegrated just like any animal. But here and there we find an inverse function of the phenomenon. By death, in the animal, the radial is reabsorbed into the tangential, while in man it escapes and is liberated from it. It escapes from entropy by turning back to Omega: the *hominisation* of death itself.[80]

It should be noted that Teilhard has used a philosophical assumption to verify a theological assumption; both assumptions

---

[80]*The Phenomenon of Man,* p. 272.

are scientifically unwarranted. We shall refer to the evolutionary consequences of this position when discussing Teilhard's conception of the Omega Point. For now, it is necessary to point out the ambiguity of his thought if we disregard the distinction between *radial* and *tangential* energy (Teilhard himself ultimately argued for a monistic position). If there is no distinction between the two alleged energies in the universe, then are not the "souls" of animals also immortal? Since only human beings are *persons,* we may safely assume from Teilhard's position that the intensity and centration of the psychic centers in all animals below man have not evolved to the point where these centers-of-consciousness are able to maintain their identity without a physical structure.

One may hold that the *degree* of differences between the mental faculties of the great apes and man is so great that the distinction may be referred to as one of kind. However, we must remember that the evolutionary stages of psychic development between the Miocene apes and present man are not represented by extant species but they may be inferred from the paleontological evidence which clearly shows an increase in cranial capacity in primate evolution.[81] Such a distinction between levels of consciousness and self-consciousness or reflective activity does not warrant Teilhard's assumption that there are quantum jumps or discrete discontinuities in the otherwise continuity of evolution. (There is no sudden leap from awareness to self-consciousness during the development of a child's mind, but merely a gradual increase in the awareness of one's self and the environment. We may speak of the emergence of personality.) Even if a distinction of *kind* is made between the psychic manifestations of the apes and man, it does not justify believing in the personal immortality of the human mind. Teilhard's philosophy of man, like his view

---

[81]We may safely infer from the paleontological evidence that the trend in primate evolution towards increased cranial capacity represents a quantitative and qualitative change in the brain itself. For an explanation of the evolution of the brain and its relationship to mental activity, see C. Judson Herrick: *The Evolution of Human Nature.* New York, Harper and Brothers, 1956.

of the cosmos, is religiously oriented. Had he not had to reconcile his evolutionary perspective with the dogmas of the Catholic Church, his philosophical anthropology would certainly have been different.

The conceptions of man have changed throughout history. To a large extent, this has been due to the increase of scientific knowledge (all thought is historically and socially conditioned). Aristotle represented the epitome of Greek thought. Not only did he have the advantage of critically reflecting on the pre-Socratics and Plato, but carried out natural investigations of his own. He taught a biologically oriented view of man and the universe. Man was a rational animal, a terrestrial microcosm that imperfectly mirrored the Unmoved Mover. Had he not been influenced by Plato's dogmatic doctrine of the fixity of Forms, Aristotle might have discovered the fluidity of species.

The Church taught that man was an incarnate spirit, i.e. man's body participated in the temporal, imperfect, immanent world of changing nature or Becoming while his mind or soul participated in the eternal, perfect, transcendent world of unchanging spirit or Being. It is unfortunate that the Church had dogmatized the philosophy of Aristotle, for it prevented further scientific inquiry which would have corrected the numerous errors in Aristotle's thought.[82]

With the Renaissance, science and philosophy were free from religious dogmatism and suppression. Investigations into the natural sciences, especially astronomy and physics, invalidated the earlier geocentric and geostatic positions. The works of Bruno and Galileo were instrumental in establishing a proper cosmology. It is unfortunate that both suffered from the dogmatism of the

---

[82]I am here referring to the philosophy of St. Thomas Aquinas which represents an attempt to reconcile Aristotelianism with Christianity. Like Aristotelianism, Thomism does not support an evolutionary perspective. This thought still continues in modern philosophy, e.g. see the writings of Jacques Maritain.

Church.[83] Nevertheless, scientific inquiry and logic were slowly replacing dogmatic faith and mysticism.

Because of the successful use of mathematics in understanding and predicting astronomical and physical phenomena in nature, e.g. the works of Galileo, Newton, and Kepler, organismic views of the universe were replaced by mechanical views. As a result, even man was held to be, at least in part, merely a very complex machine.[84]

Descartes, Spinoza, and Leibniz had presented rational models of the universe based upon mathematical methodologies. Descartes and Spinoza had employed geometrical methods. Leibniz based his metaphysics on his infinitesimal or differential calculus. This method had the advantage of enabling Leibniz to establish a process cosmology. Teilhard never relied upon mathematics, although he admired Leibniz. Concerning Albert Einstein, he wrote:

> I don't have the hundredth of the Einstein's mathematical brains. But I am dumbfounded that such a man should not realize that a single particle of consciousness present in the Universe makes it physically necessary that the Universe should become all-conscient eventually, at the end of the transformation; and what finally is Consciousness, if not Personality? . . . The trouble with Einstein, and so many others, is that they still imagine a "personal God" as a sort of super-Man, and not as the focus and center of a cosmic-personalistic Evolution. At least, I feel satisfied in observing that, by concentrating my effort on this very question of the "personalistic nature" of Universe and Evolution, I hit the exact point on which everything depends, ultimately in the present human conflict.[85]

[83]It is interesting to note that Teilhard kept a picture of Galileo in his study. Like Galielo, Teilhard was a creative innovator who was silenced by the Church.

[84]See Julien Offray De La Mettrie: *Man a Machine.* La Salle, Illinois, Open Court, 1961. La Mettrie anticipated the natural evolution of man and his soul. See pp. 100, 101, 103, 135, 140, 144.

[85]*Letters to Two Friends: 1926-1952,* p. 149. Teilhard and Einstein died in the same year, month, and vicinity. See, *Science and Synthesis.* New York, Springer-Verlag, 1971. Einstein desired to ultimately unite within one fundamental field or system of fields such different phenomena as gravitation, electromagnetism, and material entities; that all empirical laws might be expressable within

With the rise of biology in the last century, philosophers started to return to an organismic view of the universe. The theory of evolution substantiated such a turn away from the crude mechanistic models. (Teilhard wrote during the conflicts between mechanistic materialism and vitalism, science and religion.) How, then, should we view man's place in the universe?

For centuries it has been taught that man's superior mental powers were due to his participation in a rational world of Being, i.e. that man somehow bridges the "gap" between the realms of Being and Becoming. The Church had forbidden inquiry into the nature of man, holding that the human body was sacred and therefore not subject to scientific investigation. It also taught that man was endowed with a simple, immaterial, immortal soul (this position inferred an ontological dualism which only resulted in relational problems). Only within the last century have biology, anthropology, and psychology become serious areas of study. The results have been most fruitful. All scientific evidence substantiates the position that man is entirely the product of a natural evolution.

It is egocentric and anthropocentric for man to place himself on an ontological plane higher than the rest of the biological kingdom. There was no first, unique couple. Human evolution may have been monophyletic before extensive migrations from Africa, but it certainly was not monogenetic, i.e. the human phylum has not developed from a single couple. As with all other species, evolution is the evolution of *populations*. Man has descended or ascended from the Miocene hominoids (the author believes this is now an established fact). It is Teilhard's interpretation of this fact that is unwarranted. To refer to his position as a super-science, as some have done, is simply to cover the error. If anything, Teilhard's interpretation is merely super-wishful thinking.

---

one universal system of nonlinear equations for the components of this unified field theory. Such a speculation has been the dream of the rationalists.

Man is a historico-bio-psycho-social complex, a product of and totally within a physical universe. From a planetary perspective, the emergence of *Homo sapiens* is a recent, natural event. Likewise, human experience in all of its modes is a recent phenomenon within evolution. As such, the physical or natural world is independent of and prior to human experience. Such a perspective, grounded in the special sciences and given coherence by the doctrine of evolution and logic, prevents adhering to any form of idealism since mental activity is a product of a material nature and not *vice versa*.

A tremendous amount of information is known about man. In general, he is an evolved, plastic, mutable, and except for his nervous system, a general animal. His success during the past fifteen or twenty million years has been primarily due to his ability to adapt successfully to changing environments. As a result of a complex nervous system and brain, he has been able to develop language. His ability to conceptualize, and as a result use and make and own tools, has given him a superiority over the other animals and conditioned his own history.

No single characteristic distinguishes man from the great apes. Man has no eternal, fixed characteristics or permanent essence. All objects and events are subject to the *becoming* of the cosmos. Yet through the wise use of its knowledge and technology, there is no reason why the human species cannot endure indefinitely. Man is increasingly becoming capable of directing his own future evolution.

Evolution is a materialistic, multidirectional continuum. Man is a fragment of this planetary process. A broad naturalism which incorporates the knowledge of the natural, social, formal, and conceptual sciences is sufficient to explain man's place in the universe.[86] What is needed is more science supplemented by the rigorous tools of philosophy.

---

[86]Such a broad view of naturalism is clearly advocated in the writings of Marvin Farber, e.g. see *Basic Issues of Philosophy*. New York, Harper and Row, 1968, pp. 213-235.

Chapter V

TEILHARD'S OMEGA POINT

FOR TEILHARD, time is biological, organic, or evolutionary (space-time is physically diverging but spiritually converging). His thought concentrates on an analysis of planetary convergence. Through extrapolation, he extended his coherent and integrated view of the universe to include the future direction of planetary evolution. But from the same natural and social facts a plurality of interpretations may be given to the evolutionary process. In general, we have seen that such explanations are basically materialistic, vitalistic, or spiritualistic. For Teilhard, cosmic evolution is irreversible and moving antientropically toward greater conscious unity. (This, he argues, is the inevitable result of *radial* energy.) Let us now consider Teilhard's vision of the future development and end of human evolution.

A. THE DEVELOPMENT OF TEILHARD'S OMEGA POINT

Teilhard's mature thought was less interested in the geological and paleontological evidences for evolution, but more concerned with the future survival, direction, and goal of human progress. He had always maintained that naturalism was necessary but not sufficient to provide an adequate interpretation of planetary evolution. Neo-Darwinism or the Synthetic Theory of Evolution, which adds the understanding of population genetics to supplement the positive principles of Darwinism (i.e. natural selection or differential reproduction, sexual selection, and artificial selection or domestication), is incomplete for it neglects the religious element of human existence in general and psycho-social evolution in particular. Evolution is a condition of all of the phenomena in the universe, but biological principles should not be extended to interpret the entire cosmic process. Teilhard resorted to theological and philosophical assumptions to supplement scientific evidence. Like Whitehead, he saw the universe in general, and the earth in particular, as an organism:

> As you know, I believe that the World is an immense plastic thing subject to the influence of Spirit.[1]

> It has a birth, a development, and presumably a death ahead.[2]

If planetary evolution is spiritual, as Teilhard maintained it was, then it necessarily requires a spiritual end. He stressed that for survival, a collective mankind must supplement science with a belief in progress, unity, and a *personal* God.

Within this organismic and spiritual framework, Teilhard focused upon the human phylum. Man is unique because he is the only animal that is self-conscious, i.e. man knows that he knows, whereas animals merely know. (We have already discussed Teilhard's argument for man's uniqueness in the universe.) In man, consciousness has been raised to the second power, i.e. consciousness in man has involuted back upon itself so that it has become an object of its own awareness. The human brain folding or convoluting back upon itself has resulted in the ability of thought to reflect upon itself. As we have seen, this represented a qualitative leap in biological evolution. Another planetary "mutation" had taken place, resulting in a new transformation—the eventual formation of a single, unbroken, global tissue, membrane, or network of reflective consciousness and its products, i.e. the noosphere.

Likewise, during the past thousands of years of cultural evolution or the socialization of man, the human species has remained a biological unit. That is to say, man as a genus has not speciated out as other plants and animals have done over long periods of time but has, due to his uniqueness and global finitude, begun to converge upon himself. Like geogenesis and biogenesis, but even more so, noogenesis is a single, unitary process. Teilhard points out that conscious reflection or personalization and planetary reflexion or planetization are the two aspects of the *phenomenon* of man.

Teilhard argued that man is still incomplete:

[1]*Letters to Two Friends: 1926-1952*, p. 78.
[2]*The Phenomenon of Man*, p. 101.

Consequently man is, at least provisionally, the ultimate stage of an evolution which could not be understood without a biased progress of the universe towards higher and higher cerebro-psychic levels.[3] No proof exists that Man has come to the end of his potentialities, that he has reached his highest point. On the contrary, everything suggests that at the present time we are entering a peculiarly critical phase of super-humanisation.[4]

In a general sense, hominization has been the progressive phyletic spiritualization of the human layer. But the evolution of man or hominization is unfinished. Super-hominization of the human layer is resulting from the noosphere closing in upon itself as a result of continued noogenesis upon the finite sphericity of the earth. Thoughts are encircling the earth as a psychic membrane. And for Teilhard, *persons* grow through increased knowledge obtained from a social milieu. Nietzsche had also maintained that man is incomplete in actualizing his potentialities, but emphasized the free, creative individual independent from social suppression. We may generalize by saying that the difference between Nietzsche and Teilhard on this point is the distinction between developing individuality or personality respectively. Differing from Nietzsche, Teilhard held that: "No evolutionary future awaits man except in association with all other men."[5]

Teilhard saw cultural evolution as the extension of biological evolution. He held that the axis of biogenesis culminated in a new genesis, *a unity of movement* toward *super-life* or *neo-life,* i.e. the personalization of evolution. Psycho-social evolution manifested itself in two phases. First, the socialization of expansion or divergence represented by the Paleolithic and Mesolithic stages of cultural evolution. For two million years man evolved and migrated, spreading himself literally around the earth (Teilhard referred to this process as planetization, i.e. man covering the planet as a biological unit). Second, and following this bio-social divergence of the human layer, planetization is culminating in the global socialization of compression or convergence started during the "Neolithic Metamorphosis," i.e. during the last ten thousand

---

[3]*The Appearance of Man*, pp. 130-131.
[4]*The Future of Man*, p. 113.
[5]*The Phenomenon of Man*, p. 246.

years. As a result of this bio-social convergence, the modern earth is experiencing acculturation and miscegenation on a planetary scale.[6] Teilhard, always optimistic, held that planetary senescence and/or death were impossible. Since bio-social evolution was inevitable, he envisioned an ultimate humanized earth:

> And, really, quite seriously speaking, I don't see how we can escape the alternative: either the world is developing, through good and bad chances, something "adorable," and then we must serve and love it; or it is simply absurd, and then we must reject it as much as we can.[7]

> Under the combined efforts of science, morality, and association in society, some super-mankind is emerging; and it is very probably in the direction of Spirit that we should look, if we wish to know what form it will take.[8]

When studying cultural phenomena, anthropologists may emphasize different aspects. Ethnological studies may be concerned with structuralism,[9] functionalism, or configurationalism (the relationship between cultures and personality developments). There has been a recent revival of the theory of cultural evolution in anthropological literature[10] (one recalls the work of Spencer,

---

[6]Teilhard stressed that the human "races" or genetic populations complemented each other during global acculturation and miscegenation. No one population was superior to the others.

[7]*Letters to Two Friends: 1926-1952*, p. 175.

[8]*Writings in Time of War*, p. 38.

[9]For a recent concern for structuralism in social anthropology with philosophical considerations, see the works of Claude Lévi-Strauss. For an excellent survey of the history of anthropological theory, see Marvin Harris: *The Rise of Anthropological Theory*. New York, Crowell, 1970.

[10]For recent literature on the evolution of culture see V. Gordon Childe's *Man Makes Himself* (1961), *Social Evolution* (1963), and *What Happened in History* (1965); Margaret Mead's *Continuities in Cultural Evolution* (1964); Marshall D. Sahlins and Elman R. Service's *Primitive Social Organization: An Evolutionary Perspective* (1964); and Leslie A. White's *The Science of Culture: A Study of Man and Civilization* (1949) and *The Evolution of Culture: The Development of Civilization to the Fall of Rome* (1959). In general, cultural evolution exhibits technological progress resulting in increased specialization in labor accompanied by greater complexity in politico-social organization. Technologically, we may speak of the osteodontokeratic, paleolithic, mesolithic, neolithic, i.e. copper, bronze, and iron ages, industrial, and atomic stages. Socially, we have bands (hunters, gatherers, and fishers), tribes and chiefdoms (horticul-

Tylor, and Morgan in the last century). From his planetary perspective, Teilhard offers an historico-phenomenology of cultural evolution. (We have noted that the noosphere represents the latest structure of planetary evolution, and that it manifests two sequential phases.) He resorted to a Lamarckian interpretation of cultural evolution, emphasizing the accumulation of knowledge and technology from generation to generation. As a crucial part of noogenesis, technology is progressing, accelerating, and converging. It complements the biological and conscious convergence of the human species. As a result of the acceleration of psychosocial evolution with its accumulation of knowledge and technology (a phenomenon aided by the limited roundness of the earth which forces acculturation), Teilhard was aware that it would be feasible, through euthenics and eugenics,[11] for man to control and improve his own future evolution. In short, man himself could direct the process of super-hominization:

> By reflecting on itself in man, evolution does not therefore merely become conscious of itself. It becomes at the same time to some extent capable of directing and accelerating itself also.[12]

Teilhard's collectivism[13] differs radically from Nietzsche's individ-

---

ture and agriculture), and industrial nations. Teilhard acknowledged this, but generalized the whole process into the two planetary stages: (a) socialization of divergence followed by (b) socialization of convergence. For Teilhard, psychosocial evolution will culminate in the global collectivity of mankind.

[11]Euthenics is the improvement of the human species through environmental and educational means, while eugenics (a term coined by Sir Francis Galton in 1883) is the improvement of the human species through an application of the understanding of the hereditary principles of genetics.

[12]*The Appearance of Man*, p. 254.

[13]There are important similarities between Teilhardism and Marxism, although the differences are greater. Both originated from a historico-natural attitude, emphasized humanism and the value of a collective mankind, and expressed a deep concern for the survival and improvement of the human condition. But Teilhard saw the present human condition resolved only by eliminating the present alienation between mankind and a personal God through the increase of love (the amorization of the human phylum) and further converging evolution towards global unanimization of the noosphere. The Marxists, of course, could not accept his theological orientation. Yet it is ironical that many Marxists have been more sympathetic and receptive to Teilhard's thought than the Jesuit order. Like their treatment of Hegel, the Marxists simply need to turn Teilhard's system upsidedown.

ualism. Nietzsche had rejected Christianity, Democracy, and Utilitarianism, but held to the doctrine of evolution. He envisioned the appearance of the superman or overman as a result of further moral and intellectual development (a chosen few would evolve beyond the present flock or herd morality of the masses) :

> Man is something that shall be overcome. . . . Behold, I teach you the overman. The overman is the meaning of the earth. . . . Man is a rope, tied between beast and overman—a rope over an abyss.[14]

> Man hitherto—as it were, an embryo of the man of the future;—all the form-giving forces directed toward the latter are present in the former. . . . I write for a species of man that does not yet exist: for the "masters of the earth." . . . The highest men live beyond the rulers, freed from all bonds; and in the rulers they have their instruments. . . . Not "mankind" but *overman* is the goal![15]

For Nietzsche, man is the most cunning, courageous, delicate, and interesting of the animals, as well as the most unfortunate and cruelest. But unfinished man would become *complete!* He taught that in sharp contrast to the mediocre man with his "slave morality," there will emerge the artistically creative, independent higherman or overman who will be "beyond good and evil." The "human, all-too-human" majority will be surpassed by the superhuman affirmation of life manifested in the chosen minority. But where Nietzsche spoke of the superman, Teilhard taught of a super-humanity. He held that a super-humanity could only emerge through a Christian collectivity. Unlike Nietzsche, Teilhard taught that God is not dead but merely above and ahead of Christogenesis.[16] Within the noosphere, evolution continues to

---

[14]Nietzsche: *The Portable Nietzsche,* pp. 124, 125, 126.

[15]Nietzsche: *The Will to Power,* pp. 365, 503, 519.

[16]As a Jesuit-priest, Christianity played a very important part in Teilhard's evolutionary philosophy. He saw the "Christian phenomenon" as a continuation of psycho-social evolution. Through the influence of Christianity, noogenesis was extending itself into a Christogenesis; cosmic evolution or cosmogenesis is Christocentric. Teilhard's religious position is general and broad enough to include all Christian faiths, provided they believe in converging evolution. We shall see that Christianity plays an important role in uniting the human phylum through its emphasis on love; Teilhard held that love, which exists throughout all levels of evolution, is the highest form of *radial* energy.

progress forward and upward although the movement may be almost imperceptible.

Teilhard envisioned a "Human Front" with faith in Futurism, Universalism, and Personalism. Since Democracy, Communism, and Totalitarianism had their strengths *and* weaknesses, he taught that only Christianity was capable of guiding spiritual evolution to its completion. Only Christianity is capable of saving the *person,* in contrast to the individual, within a collectivity, as well as acknowledging the primacy of *spirit.*[17] Likewise, he taught that Christianity replaces pessimism and the passivity of isolated individuals with optimism and the activity of collective *persons.* The end of Christogenesis is the formation of a collective Super-humanity manifesting hyper-reflection. Christ is no longer merely a historical figure. Instead, Christ takes on a cosmic and dynamic dimension. If the author understands Teilhard correctly, his mystical vision was bold enough to identify a dynamic Christ with cosmic evolution! As a result, Teilhard presents a universal and evolutive Christ:

> The Communion of Saints is held together in the hallowed unity of a physically organized Whole; and this Whole—more absolute than the individuals over which it has dominion, in as much as the elements penetrate into and subsist in God as a *function* of Him and not as isolated particles—this Whole is the Body of *Christ.* . . . The mystical Body of Christ should, in fact, be conceived as a physical Reality, *in the strongest sense the words can bear.* . . . Christ has a *cosmic Body* that extends throughout the whole universe: such is the final proposition to be borne in mind.[18]

> By the Universal Christ, I mean Christ the organic centre of the entire universe. . . . Christ, we must add, is the plenitude of the universe, its principle of synthesis.[19]

Through Christ, evolution is holy. Through love-energy, the

---

[17]From Without a human being is merely an individual, but from a consideration of the Within he is a *person.* Although a human being may lose his individuality within a collectivity, he increases his personality. Once again, Teilhard's position results from his giving consciousness a privileged postion. The "cosmic" Law of centro-Complexity-Consciousness was his only parameter.

[18]*Writings in Time of War,* pp. 49, 51, 58.

[19]*Science and Christ,* pp. 14, 33.

highest form of *radial* energy, the consummation of the world will be brought about.

But what about the present human condition? Teilhard taught that the anguish of modern man, who fears the possibility of total death, is caused by an awareness of the enormity of space, time and number. The scientific discoveries of the past centuries, especially the theory of evolution, have jarred the human mind from its geocentric, geostatic, and nonevolutionary orientation. The meaning and purpose of human existence was being questioned, and forms of existentialism dominated intellectual circles.[20] For Teilhard, the answer was still to be found in Christianity. He taught that only love was capable of fulfilling and completing noogenesis, which we have seen to be nothing more or less than a Christogenesis. The survival of mankind required an increase in scientific knowledge *and love.* He taught that the cosmic energy of love, which is everywhere in the universe in some extenuated form, is capable of preserving and perfecting that which it unites. Christianity represents a phylum of love. Christogenesis is the increase of *radial* energy, now in the form of love-energy, and the decrease of *tangential* energy:

> Only love has the power of moving being.[21]
>
> Spiritualized Energy is the flower of Cosmic Energy.[22]
>
> All conscious energy is, like love (and because it is love), founded on hope.[23]

Schopenhauer's will-to-live and Nietzsche's will-to-power have been replaced by Teilhard's will-to-love. Through love-energy, cosmic evolution represents a *divinizing convergence.*

For Teilhard, human survival and fulfillment demands a superior form of existence. He held that the ultimate *source* and object of love is above and ahead of the evolutionary process. It is not something but a supreme Someone, the Great Presence or

---

[20]Unlike Sartre, Kafka, and Camus, Teilhard saw man's present precarious situation resolved in a return to theism; his position is similar to the religious views of Buber, Marcel, and Blondel.

[21]*Writings in Time of War*, p. 200.

[22]*Building the Earth*, p. 71.

[23]*The Phenomenon of Man*, p. 232.

Great Stability. In short, the ultimate object of love can only be a *personal* God:

> The only possible Motive Power of a life which has reached the stage of Reflection is an Absolute, or in other words a Divine, Term.[24]

> In the centre, so glaring as to be disconcerting, is the uncompromising affirmation of a personal God: God as providence, directing the universe with loving, watchful care; and God the revealer, communicating himself to man on the level of and through the ways of intelligence.[25]

It is very important to note Teilhard's distinction between God-Omega and the Omega Point. Unfortunately Teilhard himself is not always careful to point out this significant distinction. God-Omega is the transcendent focus and end of the personalizing universe (i.e. God-Omega is the Personal Center of universal convergence), while the Omega Point is the final event of planetary evolution. God-Omega is the Center of centers, the highest and unique Monad. In fact, the evolutionary process itself is sustained by this *Prime Mover ahead,* the ultimate Gatherer and Consolidator. What are the characteristics of this ultimate Monad that supports the evolution of the universe? Teilhard held that autonomy, actuality, irreversibility, and transcendence are the four attributes of God-Omega. Being *already in existence* as provider and revealer, God-Omega is directing, unifying, and purifying the personalizing and converging cosmogenesis which, through love, is extended into a Christogenesis which will be fulfilled at the Omega Point:

> By virtue of the convergence of the cosmic lines, as I have said, we must surmise the existence of a higher centre of consciousness ahead of us, at the apogee of Evolution. But if we seek to determine the position and analyse the properties of this Supreme Centre it soon becomes clear that we must look far beyond and far above any mere aggregation of perfected Mankind. If it is to be capable of joining together in itself the prolonged fibres of the world, the apex of the cone within which we move can be conceived only as something that is ultra-conscious, ultra-personalized, ultra-present.[26]

---

[24]*Building the Earth,* p. 59.
[25]*The Phenomenon of Man,* p. 293.
[26]*The Future of Man,* p. 92.

We think of Leibniz when Teilhard tells us that God-Omega is an indestructible, distinct Center radiating at the core of a system of centers, i.e. the Absolute Mind at the center of a system of centers-of-consciousness. We are also told that God-Omega is transcendent and immanent, as well as the Efficient and Final Cause of cosmic Evolution. In short, Teilhard adopted the position of panentheism.[27] God-Omega does not "make" things but makes things make themselves by being immanent in cosmic evolution as Christ, the vital principle or Force, and transcendent as the Final Cause:

> God, who is as immense and all-embracing as matter, and at the same time as warm and intimate as a soul, is the Centre who spreads through all things. . . . God is at work within life. He helps it, raises it up, gives it the impulse that drives it along, the appetite that attracts it, the growth that transforms it. . . . God, the personal and loving Infinite, is the Source, the motive Force and the End of the Universe. . . . The world came from God, to return enriched and purified to God. Such is the design of the universe. . . . In very truth, it is God, and God alone whose Spirit stirs up the whole mass of the universe in ferment.[28]

The concept of an Omega Point is Teilhard's original but most vulnerable assumption. We saw that planetary evolution is ultimately an anthropogenesis, i.e. a preparation for the emergence of man. Hominization, the actual evolution of man, is now extending itself into a super-hominization through Christogenesis. Or from the theological perspective, cosmogenesis is the emer-

---

[27]One thinks of Arsitotle's four causes, but with Teilhard, the Efficient, Material, Formal, and Final causes are eventually united into one Supreme Center, God-Omega; cosmic history is multiplicity proceeding towards unity. Aristotelianism is not evolutionary or monistic (a Platonic influence). Teilhard's panentheism was anticipated by another mystic, Plotinus. Plotinus held that nature manifested hypostases, realms, or *spheres* which emanated or effulgurated from the One; the spheres are Mind, Life, and Matter or the Void. His system is dynamic and cyclical. In short, Teilhard's evolutionary panentheism is not Platonic or Aristotelian, but a recent form of neo-Platonism. As a mystic, he was primarily concerned with *unity;* the dualistic natures of Platonism and Aristotelianism prevent a monistic interpretation of reality. For a more recent similarity, we have Whitehead's distinction between the Primordial and Consequent natures of God. See Alfred North Whitehead: *Process and Reality: An Essay in Cosmology.* New York, Harper and Row, 1960, pp. 519-533.

[28]*Writings in Time of War*, pp. 48, 61, 81, 130.

gence of the cosmic Christ. The Mystical Body of Christ is literally the collectivity of all souls or monads that have, are, and will emerge within evolution. With noogenesis, the planet is acquiring a "brain" and "heart." Extended to its logical conclusion, Teilhard taught that the earth will acquire a *single* Mind and a *single* Heart which will become united in one *single* Center. Remembering that Teilhard envisioned evolution as a pyramid, spiral, or cone, the process is now narrowing and converging upon an apex which is the Omega Point. The union of a super-conscious mankind on a planetary scale is to be followed by its union with a personal God, i.e. God-Omega. (This final union is the apogee of evolution. In short, after the geosphere, biosphere, and noosphere, there will be formed one last structure, the theosphere.)

We have already seen that in Teilhard's thought man differs in *kind* from the other animals, and as a result of this psychic or *radial* energy is qualitatively different. He assumed that the death of a *person* merely liberated an immortal center-of-consciousness. For thousands of years since the first reflective beings died this side of the last critical threshold between Life and Thought, all such liberated reflective monads have been forming a planetary layer of thought. Hominization extended in super-hominization is finalized in a *mega-synthesis* or super-arrangement of persons, forming a unified, harmonized super-consciousness around the finite spherical geometry of the earth:

> Thus through the combined influence of two curves, both cosmic in nature—one physical (the roundness of the earth) and one psychic (the reflective's self-attraction), Mankind is now caught up, as though in a train of gears, at the heart of a continually accelerating vortex of self-totalisation.[29]

For Teilhard, the Omega Point is an inevitable, extra-planetary event, i.e. the final paroxysm of evolution which will transcend time and space. The "Principle of Emergence" is extended to its limit in the formation of a conscious Pole, a "Soul of souls" as the result of a super-centration of persons into an absolutely

---

[29]*Man's Place in Nature*, pp. 99-100.

original Person or single Supreme Center. In turn, this aggregate of persons involutes or converges onto God-Omega.

Teilhard had held that everything that rises must converge, and that fuller being is closer union. The Omega Point, then, represents the final, creative, differentiated union as a result of a converging cosmogenesis. With the attainment of the Omega Point, Teilhard's law of the recurrence of creative unions is manifested for the last time. He taught that evolution unites like to like. With the Omega Point, we have the ultimate synthesis in which the Universal and Personal fuse as the result of the interior totalization of the *spirit of the earth:*

> . . . ahead of, or rather in the heart of, a universe prolonged along its axis of complexity, there exists a divine centre of convergence. That nothing may be prejudged, and in order to stress its synthesising and personalising function, let us call it the *point Omega.* Let us suppose that from this universal centre, this Omega point, there constantly emanate radiations hitherto only perceptible to those persons whom we call "mystics." Let us further imagine that, as the sensibility or response to mysticism of the human race increases with planetisation, the awareness of Omega becomes so widespread as to warm the earth psychically while physically it is growing cold. Is it not conceivable that Mankind, at the end of its totalisation, its folding-in upon itself, may reach a critical level of maturity where, leaving Earth and stars to lapse slowly back into the dwindling mass of primordial energy, it will detach itself from this planet and join the one true, irreversible essence of things, the Omega point! A phenomenon perhaps outwardly akin to death: but in reality a simple metamorphosis and arrival at the supreme synthesis. An escape from the planet, not in space or outwardly, but spirtually and inwardly, such as the hyper-centration of cosmic matter upon itself allows.[30]

This is Teilhard's vision of the end of the world. Philosophically, he argues that its consummation is the collective responsibility of all human effort through love. Theologically, he maintains that the ultimate success of the future evolution of the human phylum is guaranteed by God:

> For a Christian believer it is interesting to note that the final success of hominisation (and thus cosmic involution) is positively guaran-

---

[30]*The Future of Man*, pp. 122-123.

teed by the "redeeming virtue" of the God incarnate in his creation. But this takes us beyond the plan of phenomenology.[31]

But what about the present state of the earth?

There were the first men—those who witnessed our origin. There are
others who will witness the great scenes of the end. To us, in our
brief span of life, falls the honour and good fortune of coinciding
with a critical change of the noosphere.[32]

In short, Teilhard has given us a simple argument in natural
theology, i.e. if cosmic evolution is spiritualistic, directional, and
converging, then it can only terminate in a Personal Center of
ultimate complexity and consciousness. (It is obvious that we
have not been dealing solely with a scientific treatise.) The Omega
Point represents his most daring assertion. By repeatedly referring to theologically oriented philosophical assumptions and mysticism, he has not limited himself to a rigorous historico-phenomenological interpretation of planetary evolution.

B. THE PROBLEM OF EVIL

Teilhard did admit, however, that there may also be an evolution of evil (there seemed to be an excess of evil in the world as it
is). He made the common distinction between physical and moral
evil, but essentially there was only one form:

Physical and moral evil *are produced by the process of Becoming:*
everything that evolves has its own sufferings and commits its own
faults.[33]

There is *only one Evil*—disunity. We call it "moral" when it affects
the free zones of the soul. But even then (like Good, moreover, which
"unites") it is still *physical in essence.*[34]

Evil is "matter," determinism, multiplicity, and death. It is that
which prevents evolution towards creative union. However,
growth itself necessitates evil. The evolution of the universe rep-

---

[31]*The Phenomenon of Man*, p. 308n.

[32]*Ibid.*, p. 214. Consistent with his thought, the last critical threshold results in
the formation of the theosphere; the last manifestation of teleological evolution
—the fulfillment of the Law of centro-Complexity-Consciousness.

[33]*Writings in Time of War*, p. 71.

[34]*Science and Christ*, p. 80n.

resents an infinite number of steps from absolute evil, i.e. total nothingness or total plurality, to the Supreme Good, which is total being or total unity. Evolution is the progressive movement from absolute plurality to absolute unity, i.e. from imperfection to perfection. In short, evil is a result of the privation of God-Omega, for God-Omega is perfect unity.

In *The Phenomenon of Man,* Teilhard briefly discusses the evils of disorder and failure, solitude and anxiety, and growth.[35] Evil is a necessary element of cosmic evolution proceeding by trial and error (i.e. directed chance) in its organization from multiplicity to unity. Cosmic History is the movement from heterogeneity to homogeneity.

From this perspective, the traditional doctrine of Original Sin, like the doctrine of the Incarnation, takes on a cosmic dimension. The Fall is no longer an historical event, but a general condition of cosmic History. Original Sin, i.e. finitude or death due to the disintegration of structure, affects and infects everything in the Universe. It is a general condition affecting the totality of the spatio-temporal organicity of the Universe as a result of the atomicity (statistical disorder) and organicity (incompleteness) of the Universe. In short, Teilhard taught that sin or evil has a trans-historical or pan-cosmic character, and is structurally *inevitable* within an imperfect, i.e. unfinished, Evolution (in cosmogenesis, the Creation, Incarnation, and Redemption represent three complementary phases of the same single process).

If evil continues to increase, an alternative that Teilhard acknowledged, then the end of the world will represent a bifurcation of the noosphere. An internal schism of the noosphere will result in a polarity between the love of the physical and the love of the spiritual. As a result, only that percentage of the noosphere which has synthesized itself across space, time, and evil will be united to God-Omega at the Omega Point. The remaining monads will, presumably, continue to exist but in a state of suffering for they are excluded from the presence of God-Omega.

From the theological perspective *radial* energy is God's love,

---

[35]*The Phenomenon of Man,* pp. 311-313. In short, evil is statistically inevitable as a by-product of evolution.

His creative Spirit which both vitalizes the cosmos from *within* while divinely attracting directional evolution from *above*. (We have seen that the evolution of the universe is ultimately the development of the cosmic Christ.) The universe emanated from God-Omega, is evolving, and will inevitably return to God-Omega at the Omega Point (God is both God-Alpha and God-Omega, the Beginning and End of Reality). This position retains the Christian doctrine of the Trinity. God is three distinct persons within a single unity: the Father is God-Omega; the Son is the "physical" universe; the Holy Spirit is the vital principle of love-energy.

Teilhard had taught that:

> Mankind, born on this planet and spread over its entire surface, coming gradually to form around its earthly matrix a single, major organic unity, enclosed upon itself; a single, hyper-complex, hyper-centrated, hyper-conscious arch-molecule, co-extensive with the heavenly body on which it was born. Is not this what is happening at the present time—the closing of this spherical, thinking circuit?[36]

We have seen that the outcome or epitome of this developing superorganism is the unity of mankind manifested at the Omega Point. But Teilhard's alleged cosmic perspective is actually geocentric or planetary in orientation. Nowhere does he seriously anticipate the possibility that human progress may continue beyond the present confines of the earth. For Teilhard, the colonization of other planets in our solar system as well as journeys to the other stars, i.e. intergalactic travel, are held to be untenable. Yet for a mind that thought in billions of years and held that man's psycho-social progress would continue to accelerate for thousands of years to come, it is astonishing that he never allowed for the possibility of human divergence on a solar or cosmic scale. Kant and Hegel had recognized the philosophical significance of the finite sphericity of the earth, but for Teilhard it is of primary importance. Actually his whole system of converging evolution would collapse if man extended his evolution beyond the confines of this planet. Such a concept of divergence is Bergsonian. If we take Bergson's position seriously, which the author submits is

---

[36]*The Future of Man*, p. 115.

a more realistic position, then Teilhard's conception of an Omega Point can never be realized, or at least postponed indefinitely. The finite cosmologies of Spencer, Nietzsche, and Teilhard restrict man's development to an inevitable limit. To read these authors is to experience the suffocating perspective of a closed, finite world. No *a priori* closure should be dogmatically placed upon scientific, philosophical, and social progress. What exhilaration one feels when Bruno teaches that man is a part of an eternal and infinite universe and therefore can enjoy actualizing infinite possibilities! Perhaps the limits of man are the limits of his aspirations.

Teilhard admitted that perhaps other Omega Points had, are, or will be formed on planets elsewhere in the universe. This seems inevitable from his own position *if* the Law of increasing centro-Complexity-Consciousness is an *a priori* character of the universe (we have already seen that the law is merely a synthetic generalization derived from a planetary perspective). Even so, he held that communications with other Omega Points were unlikely. Again, planetary evolution is finite and closed, a result of Teilhard's concern for eschatology.

In the last analysis, God's love is the *modus operandi* and *raison d'être* of cosmic evolution in general and human evolution in particular.[37] Although other evolutionists have also written within a theistic framework, Teilhard's conception of an Omega Point is original.

C. RELIGIOUS INTERPRETATIONS IN THE EVOLUTIONARY LITERATURE

Lamarck held that the order of existing things in evolution was the result of the will and infinite power of a Sublime Author who was also responsible for the existence of the universe:

---

[37]There is a striking similarity between Teilhard and Aristotle; although the latter was not an evolutionist, both held to teleological interpretations of nature. Aristotle taught that the transcendent presence of the Unmoved Mover caused the directional development of terrestrial organisms as well as the circular motion of celestial objects. In short, the Unmoved Mover moved the objects of the finite but eternal universe by being the ultimate object of their degrees of desire.

Nature is herself only the general and immutable order created everywhere by this Sublime Author; she is the sum total of the general and special laws to which that order is subject. . . . I prefer to think that the whole of nature is only an effect: hence, I imagine and like to believe in a First Cause or, in short, a Supreme Power which brought nature into existence and made it such as it is.[38]

He did not elaborate on his argument for the existence of a Supreme Mind from the alleged order or design in Nature. He simply held that evolution was God's simple method of creating Nature, although its purpose was known to Him alone.

Wallace was more explicit in his theistic orientation. (We have seen that he defended Darwinism, but maintained that it wasn't sufficient to interpret cosmic evolution.) In *The World of Life* (1910), he clearly replaced naturalism with teleology, vitalism, and spiritualism:

. . . beyond all the phenomena of nature and their immediate causes and laws there is Mind and Purpose; and that the ultimate purpose is (so far as we can discern) the development of mankind for an enduring spiritual existence. . . . We may look upon our Universe, in all its parts and during its whole existence, as slowly but surely marching onwards to a predestined end. . . . This world of ours *is* the best of all *possible worlds calculated to bring about this result*. . . . The infinite Deity not only designed the whole of the cosmos, but that himself alone is the consciously acting power in every cell of every living thing that is or ever has been upon the earth. . . . The vast whole is therefore a manifestation of his power —perhaps of his very self.[39]

Although Darwin and Huxley remained agnostics, Wallace advocated theism. He clearly anticipated Teilhard's belief in the reconciliation of science and Christian faith within an evolutionary perspective. Logically speaking from a process orientation, Bruno, Leibniz, and Wallace argued that this was the *best of all possible worlds* (Teilhard had simply held that the universe was perfecting itself as it proceeded towards unity).

---

[38]Lamarck: *Zoological Philosophy*, pp. 60, 183-184. See also pp. 36, 40-41, 55, 180, 236, 342, 379.

[39]Alfred Russel Wallace: *The World of Life*. New York, Moffat, Yard and Co., 1916, pp. 299, 300, 426.

As has been noted, Fiske's "Cosmic Philosophy," unlike Spencer's "Synthetic Philosophy," took on a theistic interpretation of Nature (the "Unknowable Force" of Spencer's position was held by Fiske to be the Christian God). His view of evolution acquired a teleological and anthropocentric orientation. In *The Destiny of Man* (1884), he wrote:

> . . . he who has mastered the Darwinian theory, he who recognizes the slow and subtle process of evolution as the way in which God makes things come to pass, must take a far higher view. . . . I believe it has been fully shown that so far from degrading Humanity, or putting it on a level with the animal world in general, the doctrine of evolution shows us distinctly for the first time how the creation and the perfecting of Man is the goal toward which Nature's work has been tending from the first. . . . From the first dawning of life we see all things working together toward one mighty goal, the evolution of the most exalted spiritual qualities which characterize Humanity.[40]

Like Teilhard, Fiske held that the:

> . . . psychical development of Man is destined to go on in the future as it has gone on in the past.[41]

In *Through Nature to God* (1899), he stressed the incompleteness of human evolution:

> The genesis of humanity was by no means yet completed, but an enormous gulf had been crossed. . . . Gods' highest work is never perfected save in the fullness of time.[42]

Lamarck, Wallace, and Fiske had held to the existence of a Christian God as a result of the alleged direction of evolution manifested from the protozoans to the emergence of rational man. But they had merely stated their positions without giving systematic arguments and thoroughly considering the necessary assumptions and unverifiable implications resulting from their views. They simply represent early attempts at reconciliation which lacked rigorous philosophical and theological thinking. They are of historical significance, for their efforts illustrate that a

---

[40]Fiske: *The Destiny of Man*, pp. 32, 107, 113-114.
[41]*Ibid.*, p. 72.
[42]Fiske: *Through Nature to God*, pp. 84, 122.

materialistic interpretation of evolution was not going to easily dethrone the traditional Christian *Weltanschauung*. It was Teilhard's advantage to be educated in science, philosophy, and theology. As a result, he holds a unique place among philosophers of evolution.

Royce, Bergson, Alexander, and Morgan had presented systematic interpretations of evolution with different degrees of religious overtones. In the Kantian tradition, Royce's "Synthetic Idealism" had distinguished between the scientific description of the natural appearances of things and historical, synthetic reality which "extends infinitely beyond our private consciousness, because it is the world of an universal mind;" the latter realm "is such stuff as ideas are made of."[43] As a result of this idealistic interpretation, he held that cosmic evolution represents a rational unity. Reality is a supreme, infinite, eternal, personal Self, Absolute, or divine Logos:

> There is, then, at last, but one Self, organically, reflectively, consciously inclusive of all the selves, and so of all truth. I have called this self, Logos, problem-solver, all-knower.[44]

Although Royce's evolutionary position is idealistic, organismic, and teleological, it differs from Teilhard's view in at least two significant ways. First, Royce's view is pantheistic. The Absolute is not ontologically transcendent but the organic collectivity of all spirits, i.e. centers of appreciative consciousness. In short, God is an Absolute Person because He is the eternal collectivity of all morally evolving individuals or persons *hic et nunc:*

> The one lesson of our entire course has thus been the lesson of the unity of finite and of infinite, of temporal dependence, and of eternal significance, of the World and all its Individuals, of the One and the Many, of God and Man. . . . God's life is the infinite whole that includes this endless temporal process, and that consciously surveys it as one life, God's own life.[45]

Teilhard's view is panentheistic, for God is both a transcendent personal Center as well as the collectivity of all immanent persons.

---

[43]Royce: *The Spirit of Modern Philosophy*, p. 380.
[44]*Ibid.*, p. 379.
[45]Royce: *The World and the Individual*, vol. II, pp. 417, 418.

But since the Omega Point represents a union of the immanent and transcendent natures of God, this final synthesis may be referred to as pantheistic. However, Teilhard is careful to emphasize that this pantheistic interpretation cannot be applied to the present state of the universe.

Second, Royce held that the process of evolution is eternal (here we recall the position held by Hegel, who claimed the dialectical process to be *a priori* and eternal). The existence of God is not the result of a finite process. Cosmic evolution *is* God's will endlessly expressing itself for there is no perfect end to the universe:

> Moreover there is indeed, for our doctrine, no temporal conclusion of the world's successive processes,—no one temporal goal of evolution,—no single temporal event to which the whole creation moves.[46]

Unlike Royce, Teilhard held that cosmic evolution is goal-directed (the Omega Point will be the last event of planetary evolution, the goal of all evolutionary development).

Although Bergson's view was dualistic and divergent while Teilhard's position is monistic and convergent, there are similarities. In *Duration and Simultaneity* (1922), Bergson defended his intuitive view of duration as a single, indivisible flow of true time against Einstein's thesis of the existence of multiple, real times as a result of his theory of relativity. For Bergson, the duration of the universe includes both external time or the *élan vital* and internal time or *durée reelle*. How does Bergson's view of the cosmic unity of time resemble Teilhard's position? It must be remembered that for Bergson duration or time is absolute reality and implies consciousness. Therefore, if there is only *one* continuous time in the universe there can be only *one* stream of consciousness. He moves from an intuitive methodology to a mystical vision which resembles Teilhard's converging collectivity of centers-of-consciousness:

> All human consciousnesses are of like nature, perceive in the same way, keep in step, as it were, and live the same duration. But, nothing prevents us from imagining as many human consciousnesses as we please, widely scattered through the whole universe, but brought

---

close enough to one another for any two consecutive ones, taken at random, to overlap the fringes of their fields of outer experience. Each of these two outer experiences participates in the duration of each of the two consciousnesses. And, since the two consciousnesses have the same rhythm of duration, so must the two experiences. But the two experiences have a part in common. Through this connecting link, then, they are reunited in a single experience, unfolding in a single duration which will be, at will, that of either of the two consciousnesses. Since the same argument can be repeated step by step, a single duration will gather up the events of the whole physical world along its way; and we shall then be able to eliminate the human consciousnesses that we had at first laid out at wide intervals like so many relays for the motion of our thought; there will be nothing more than an impersonal time in which all things will pass.[47]

For Teilhard the convergence of a collective humanity increases personality as it evolves closer to the Personal Center, but Bergson did not write within such a theistic framework. In *Creative Evolution* he held that "harmony is rather behind us than before."[48] God was *not* a Personal Center but simply "unceasing life, acton, freedom."[49] Yet in *The Two Sources of Morality and Religion* (1932), Bergson held that mysticism was a higher form of knowledge than that acquired through intuition, i.e. mysticism is superior to intuition. He held, like Teilhard, that a future increase of mystics would change the world into an "open society," i.e. a progressive, flexible, mystical society with unlimited possibilities. Science and mysticism would complement one another in the improvement of the human condition. His optimism and final position, which revealed a Catholic influence, anticipates Teilhard's position:

> Men do not sufficiently realize that their future is in their own hands. Theirs is the task of determining first of all whether they want to go on living or not. Theirs the responsibility, then, for deciding if they want merely to live, or intend to make just the extra effort required for fulfilling, even on their refractory planet, the essential function of the universe, which is a machine for the making of gods.[50]

[47]Henri Bergson: *Duration and Simultaneity with Reference to Einstein's Theory*. New York, Bobbs-Merrill, 1965, pp. 46-47.

[48]Henri Bergson: *Creative Evolution*, p. 58.

[49]*Ibid.*, p. 271.

[50]Henri Bergson: *The Two Sources of Morality and Religion*. New York, Doubleday, 1935, p. 317.

For Teilhard, there was but a single God to be united with His Creation at the end of a converging cosmogenesis.

Alexander also attempted to reconcile theism and pantheism within an evolutionary framework, but the result is different. Like Bergson, Alexander gave priority to Time. He held that Time generated Space-Time. Space-Time in turn generated an order of successive, finite, empirical qualities, the latest emergent quality being consciousness. He then made a distinction between God and the deity within the emerging matrix or nisus of Space-Time. God is the infinite world or universe, Space-Time, or Motion (this is the pantheistic aspect of God). But God is dynamic, for the infinite universe is tending towards diety, i.e. God is "pregnant" with deity. What is deity? Deity is the next higher, finite, empirical quality that has yet to emerge from the productive movement or nisus of Time. Within the infinite series of levels of existence, deity is always that angelic quality next to emerge in the scheme of things. Therefore, while God is the infinite universe, deity is only a portion of God's nature. The deity to emerge will be different in *kind* not in degree from mind or spirit or personality. In short, deity is God's divine quality yet to emerge ahead of the present state of emergent evolution. God is infinitely immanent *hic et nunc* while the deity is finitely transcendent *in time.* This attempt to reconcile theism and pantheism, i.e. transcendence and immanence, is grounded in religious sentiment:

> God is, if we may use such language, the power which makes for deity. . . . God is the whole universe engaged in process towards the emergence of this new quality, and religion is the sentiment in us that we are drawn towards him, and caught in the movement of the world to a higher level of existence.[51]

Since the quality of mind or consciousness emerged from the quality of life, the divine quality of deity will emerge out of consciousness. Religious experiences are feelings for the vague future quality of deity. To use an analogy, the universe is the infinite body of God, while the future deity is His finite "mind" yet to emerge (the view is organismic and teleological). Although Alexander and Teilhard both attempted to reconcile theism and pan-

---

[51]Alexander: *Space, Time, and Deity,* vol. II, pp. 428, 429.

theism within an evolutionary framework, Alexander's metaphysical position is clearly different. In short, we have two forms of evolutionary panentheism. Alexander's God is totally immanent as the infinite universe, while Teilhard's God is the transcendent Personal Center. Likewise, Alexander's God is ultimately Time (we are reminded once again of Bergson's position), while Teilhard's God remains a Supreme Person as taught in traditional Christianity. Where Alexander held to the future emergence of God's deity, Teilhard saw cosmogenesis as a Christogenesis. A safe generalization is that Alexander's position is basically pantheistic while Teilhard's position remains basically Christian, i.e. theistic. Nevertheless, both positions are ultimately pantheistic in that God and the deity or Christ are aspects of a single unity.

Morgan's theory of emergent evolution comes closest to resembling Teilhard's position. In *Emergent Evolution* (1927), Morgan acknowledged[52] both an independent, evolving, physical world, i.e. a system of physical events, and a "God as the ultimate Source on which emergent evolution is ultimately dependent."[53] He taught that an acknowledgment of God was necessary to supplement a scientific interpretation of evolution (an ultimate synthesis of interpretation and explanation would result). God was presented as "directive Activity," "the Nisus through whose Activity emergents emerge, and the whole course of emergent evolution is directed."[54] As the Creative Source of emergent evolution, God is Efficiency, Causality, and Dependence. Like Teilhard, Morgan held that God explains not only the directive Activity *in* evolution but also that which from *above* "draws all things and all men upwards."[55] In short, God is immanent as the all-embracing Activity and transcendent as the goal of teleological evolution:

> We acknowledge God as above and beyond. But unless we also intuitively enjoy His Activity within us, feeling that we are in a measure one with Him in Substance, we can have no immediate knowledge

---

[52]By acknowledgment Morgan means a judgment whose verification lies beyond the range of such positive proof as naturalistic criticism rightly demands.

[53]Morgan: *Emergent Evolution*, p. 116.

[54]*Ibid.*, pp. 33, 36.

[55]*Ibid.*, p. 62.

of Causality or of God as the Source of our own existence and of emergent evolution.[56]

Philosophically, Morgan held that emergent evolution manifests a three-fold relatedness of involution, dependence, and correlation.[57] That these three categories are *a priori* is a judgment of natural piety, i.e. an acknowledgment. Emergent evolution recognizes creativity, i.e. the novelty of new kinds of events or relations in space-time, but the immanent Activity and transcendent Source are nowise susceptible of scientific proof. In *The Emergence of Novelty* (1933) he wrote:

> In accordance with the generalization accepted by evolutionists the historical advance of all cosmic events may be plotted on an ascending curve.[58]

Teilhard had also likened the path of cosmic evolution to a curve, but Morgan never wrote of a mystical union of the Activity and Source of evolution. However, he did refer to "Activity as Final Cause"[59] and of all the evolutionists his interpretation comes closest to anticipating Teilhard's view.

D. NATURALISTIC INTERPRETATIONS IN THE EVOLUTIONARY LITERATURE

Marx, Nietzsche, and Haeckel were not sympathetic to theistic interpretations of man's place in the universe. In fact, they explicitly rejected theism in favor of a naturalistic interpretation of evolution. Marx held that "the annulment of God is the emer-

---

[56]*Ibid.*, p. 301.

[57]Involution refers to the position that higher events involve the existence of lower events from which they have emerged, i.e. conscious events (mind) presuppose physiological events (life), and organic events (life) presuppose physicochemical events (matter); in short, no mind without life, and no life without matter. Dependence refers to the position that the existence of events also depends upon supervenient events. Involution and dependence supplement each other within the space-time continuum of emerging events. As we descend the pyramid of evolution we are concerned with dependence, and as we ascend the pyramid of evolution we are aware of involution; the coherency of evolution is guaranteed from above and below respectively. Correlation refers to the inseparable union of the physical and the psychical.

[58]Morgan: *The Emergence of Novelty*, p. 60.

[59]*Ibid.*, p. 189.

gence of theoretical humanism",[60] for religion is the opium of the people as it alienates them from their *natural* origin and social problems. He advocated a communistic society in which man was free from the alienating influences of wages, capital, social classes, religion, private property, and the state.

Nietzsche warned that:

> Whoever has theologians' blood in his veins, sees all things in a distorted and dishonest perspective to begin with.[61]

He taught that "God is dead" for the concept of God is meaningless as it never had or will have a metaphysical (i.e. an ontological) correlate. God is merely a historically and culturally conditioned *idea* having limitless interpretations.

Haeckel was very bold in his attack against the Church. He advocated a monistic pantheism to replace dogmatic theism:

> The monistic idea of God, which alone is compatible with our present knowledge of nature, recognises the divine spirit in all things. It can never recognize in God a "personal being," or, in other words, an individual of limited extension in space, or even of human form. God is everywhere. As Giordano Bruno has it: "There is one spirit in all things, and no body is so small that it does not contain a part of the divine substance whereby it is animated." Every atom is thus animated, and so is the ether; we might therefore, represent God as the infinite sum of all natural forces, the sum of all atomic forces and all ether-vibrations. . . . God is defined as "the supreme law of the universe," and the latter is represented as the "working of universal space."[62]

His science-oriented evolutionary philosophy rejected "homotheism," i.e. "attributing human shape, flesh, and blood to the gods."[63] He held that the Christian concept of a personal God "gives us the paradoxical picture of a 'gaseous vertebrate.'"[64]

---

[60]Fromm: *Marx's Concept of Man*, p. 188.

[61]Nietzsche: *The Portable Nietzsche*, p. 575.

[62]Haeckel: *Monism as Connecting Religion and Science*, pp. 78-79.

[63]Haeckel: *The Riddle of the Universe*, p. 12.

[64]*Ibid.* By the expression "gaseous vertebrate" Haeckel is referring to the invisible and personal aspects of the traditional Christian conception of God.

This *personal anthropism* was replaced by monistic pantheism:

> Pantheism teaches that God and the world are one. The idea of God is identical with that of nature or substance. . . . It follows necessarily that pantheism is *the world-system of the modern scientist.*[65]

Haeckel went so far as to describe "the papacy as the greatest swindle the world has ever submitted to."[66] His strong reaction to the dogmatism of the Church was reinforced by its refusal to acknowledge the implications of a naturalistic interpretation of biological evolution. Few natural philosophers have been as honest and persistent in their quests for truths. It is refreshing to see Haeckel's significance recognized in contemporary naturalistic thought.[67]

In short, the "natural attitude" may take a variety of philosophical positions, e.g. monistic panentheism, pantheism, agnosticism, and atheism. It is interesting to follow the development of the Church's attitude toward the doctrine of evolution. At first the Church condemned the theory of evolution, then it accepted it within a theistic framework. We may suspect that the Church will next claim to have "discovered" the true meaning of cosmic evolution in the works of Teilhard. There have already been attempts to show that Aristotle and St. Thomas Aquinas were evolutionists!

E.   FINAL INTERPRETATION

Teilhard's alleged "phenomenological attitude" is actually a religious or theological attitude, i.e. his *interpretation* of a natural, planetary process is grounded in Catholicism. He has assumed that evolution represents a converging space-time continuum, and that this universal character affects all levels of being. As a direct result, the successive stages of geogenesis, biogenesis, and noogenesis form the geosphere, biosphere, and noosphere respec-

---

[65]*Ibid.,* pp. 288, 289.

[66]Haeckel: *Last Words on Evolution,* p. 177.

[67]See Farber's *Naturalism and Subjectivism,* pp. 228, 262; *Phenomenology and Existence, p.* 170; and *Basic Issues of Philosophy,* pp. 220-222. Also, David H. DeGrood: *Haeckel's Theory of the Unity of Nature.* Boston, The Christopher Publishing House, 1965.

tively (this, of course, clearly advocates a finite, closed perspective since thought is never held to expand beyond the confines of the earth). In noogenesis, the planetization of the human phylum is the *external* manifestation of the *internal* convergence of the brain upon itself resulting in self-consciousness, i.e. the planetary reflexion of man is the external correlate of internal conscious reflection. The system is closed for Teilhard has given preference to eschatology. He taught that noogenesis will extend itself into the formation of a theosphere, the latter being the result of the convergence of the noosphere upon God. The completion of planetary evolution is held to be a final synthetic unity realized at the Omega Point.

Teilhard's view is scientifically unwarranted for it requires a spiritual monism, personal immortality, and a personal God, as well as dogmatically limiting human progress to a planetary end. The author believes Teilhard to be wrong when he maintains that Christianity is *necessary* for human survival.[68] To equate psycho-social evolution with Christogenesis is clearly a Catholic bias (if Teilhard acknowledged the possibility of similar psycho-social evolutions on other spheres he would find himself in the theologically embarrassing position of postulating a plurality of Christs).

One may speak of scientific, evolutionary, or natural humanism grounded in a natural attitude. The values of such a position are necessarily different from the values of Teilhard's Christian humanism. What *is* needed for human survival is the improvement of the environment (euthenics) as well as the improvement of the nature of man (eugenics). Teilhard held that a theological goal is necessary in order to motivate into action an otherwise meaningless process. Unfortunately, he never recognized an alternative in which man gives values to his existence as a result of rigorous reflection upon scientific knowledge, history, experience, and bio-psycho-social needs. In short, Teilhard's personal needs are not necessarily the needs of the human zoological group.

Teilhard's concern for cosmic unity is fulfilled in a mystical

---

[68]See Julian Huxley: *Religion Without Revelation,* for an evolutionary and naturalistic interpretation of religion.

vision. But one may distinguish between natural and spiritual mysticism. A naturalist may accept a form of mysticism if by mysticism one simply means an awareness of the spatio-temporal unity of the infinite and eternal universe (this position being the logical extension of the unity of one's finite knowledge and experience). However, some mystics may claim to be in direct communication with a transcendent Absolute either through subjective or transcendental meditation, or objective cosmic influences. Natural mysticism leads to a legitimate naturalistic monism, while spiritual mysticism advocates an unwarranted idealism or dualism.

Teilhard's concern for a union of the immanent and transcendent aspects of God resulted in a spiritual monism. His pantheistic position generates a one-many problem. Mystically, he argued that persons would not only retain their identity within such a spiritual union, but as a result of this synthesis they would increase their personality, i.e. psychic identity (we recall that Teilhard taught that closer union increases being; the Supreme Being would result from a supreme union). A naturalist need only distinguish between ontological monism and methodological and logical pluralism. The material unity of the universe is grounded in the special sciences, experience, and common sense.

It is wrong to assume that human evolution is meaningless without a personal God or a planetary end (eschatological wishes should not distort the sciences or limit man's possibilities). Teilhard has had to misrepresent nature in order to assume that the activity of God has a historical function in cosmic evolution.

We may speak of human fulfillment through scientific humanism. Like Xenophanes, Bruno, Spinoza, Goethe, Hegel, Haeckel, Royce, and Alexander, one may adopt a form of philosophical pantheism, i.e. one may acknowledge that "God" is identical with the eternal and infinite universe. However, there are those who hold that such a position is an emotional compromise, ambiguous, and meaningless. But the position of pantheism is merely a personal, *philosophical* concept of "God." From a *theological* orientation, pantheism is necessarily atheistic as it denies the existence of an eternal, transcendent Supreme Mind. To be sure, there are a plurality of interpretations of pantheism, e.g. Feuerbach referred to pantheism as "theological atheism." There is a need for a critical appraisal of the ontological, epistemological, ethical, and aesthetic implications of a materialistic, dynamic or evolutionary pantheism. (There may be politico-social reasons preventing scholars from explicitly advocating atheism. One need only recall the outrageous fate of Giordano Bruno.[69])

Our eyes should always remain open to the facts of reality, whether they are joyful or depressing. There are now over three billion human beings living on the earth, and this number will double within the next generation barring any major catastrophe.[70] It will take more than a mystical vision to unite on a planetary scale this mass of bio-psycho-social differentiations. Diversity generally creates greater diversity. And Teilhard himself was aware that ultra-specialization is the road to extinction. Certainly human activity should be directional if it is to be meaningful and fruitful. But the need and desire for goals neither justifies cosmic teleology nor a theological interpretation of the end of the world. At present, the directional development of a collective mankind seems unfeasible.

Considered as a biological whole on a planetary scale, the human zoological group has greatly transformed the face of the earth[71] (one may speak of the evolution of language, technology, politico-social structures, behavior, knowledge, and culture, etc.). Unfortunately, these changes are not necessarily progressive. The variables that may influence the growth of societies are staggering, e.g. wars, violence, disease, pollution, overpopulation, technological overspecialization, drugs, diminishing natural resources, disinterest in morality. To hold that human progress is inevitable is to ignore the harmful effects generated by these problems. Teil-

---

[69]See A. M. Paterson: *The Infinite Worlds of Giordano Bruno,* pp. 196-199. Dr. Paterson is to be commended for inaugurating extensive studies on Bruno in American philosophy.

[70]See Paul R. Ehrlich: *The Population Bomb.* New York, Ballantine, 1970.

[71]See Pierre Teilhard de Chardin's The Antiquity and World Expansion of Human Culture, In *Man's Role in Changing the Face of the Earth,* William L. Thomas, Jr. (Ed.). Chicago, The University of Chicago Press, 1956, for his mature, anthropological interpretation of hominization and planetization.

hard's optimism may be naive and dangerous if it blinds individuals from the urgent need for social reforms and action if man is to maintain any kind of a qualitative existence. (Nietzsche taught that struggle is necessary for growth.)

In the last analysis, Teilhard's Omega Point is a theological conception scientifically unwarranted and philosophically unconvincing (the Pleroma and Parousia have merely been given an evolutionary interpretation). His convergent orientation is already outdated in light of the possibility of interplanetary and intergalactic space travel. However, his optimism and emphasis on science, love, and collective effort for the future survival of mankind are commendable.

Chapter VI

CONCLUSION

A. THE TEILHARDIAN SYNTHESIS

FATHER Pierre Teilhard de Chardin's Catholic philosophy of evolution represents the most recent attempt to reconcile the special sciences, philosophy, theology, and mysticism into a coherent perspective of man's place in the universe. It is wrong to refer to Teilhard as primarily a scientist, philosopher, theologian, or mystic. The simple truth is that he was all four, for the synthesis of these four distinct fields of inquiry was precisely his major objective. The uniqueness of the Teilhardian synthesis is that it is so successful in incorporating these distinct levels of knowledge, although it is subject to severe criticism for established facts are held to substantiate theological assumptions through the use of religiously oriented philosophical concepts. However, the system does reflect a well integrated personality.

As a natural scientist, Teilhard was aware of the fluidity of reality. The whole cosmos was in evolution, for he taught of a cosmogenesis. To correctly understand the cosmos, everything in the universe must be placed within a converging space-time continuum. Concentrating on the planet earth, he was aware that billions of years of physico-chemical evolution or biogenesis had preceeded the emergence of thought. Pre-life, Life, and Thought represent the three major stages of planetary evolution. And all planetary phenomena could be placed within one of these stages or spheres. Psycho-social evolution or noogenesis is a recent planetary phenomenon, for man as a self-conscious tool maker had emerged only several million years ago. And Teilhard taught that the thinking membrane of the earth would continue to develop and converge for thousands of more years.

Value judgments were implied. Life is more valuable than physico-chemical structures, and thought is more valuable than biological structures. Since man is the only self-conscious animal on the planet, Teilhard argued that he was therefore necessarily the most valuable object in the universe. He held that man is the measure of all things knowable in the cosmos. In short, Teilhard's scientific investigation is ultimately grounded in anthropocentrism, and his alleged cosmic perspective is a planetary one.

Teilhard made lasting contributions to the fields of natural science. He wrote classical papers on the mammals of the lower Eocene epoch in France, Chinese geology in which he formulated and demonstrated the granification theory of continental development, and contributed to paleontology and physical anthropology. His popularizations of human paleontology stressed the philosophical as well as theological implications. It is unfortunate that he did not find the time to study geochemistry, biochemistry, and population genetics. Work in these and related fields may have modified his view to a more naturalistic position. For the mechanisms of evolution must be clearly understood if a correct interpretation of evolutionary phenomena is forthcoming.[72]

As a philosopher, Teilhard has given us his personal interpretation. He relied upon philosophical concepts not subject to verification but grounded in theological assumptions (we have already seen that his four basic philosophical concepts have been

---

[72]For a clear introduction to the mechanisms of the Synthetic Theory of Evolution, see E. Peter Volpe: *Understanding Evolution.* Dubuque, Iowa, Brown, 1967. For a modern interpretation of evolution from a scientific orientation, see Sir Julian Huxley: *Evolution in Action.* New York, The New American Library, 1961; *Evolution: The Modern Synthesis.* New York, Wiley, 1964; and *Man in the Modern World.* New York, The New American Library, 1964. Also see George Gaylord Simpson: *The Meaning of Evolution.* New York, The New American Library, 1959. An understanding of population genetics is necessary to understand organic evolution. A major breakthrough in genetics came with the discovery of the structure of the DNA molecule. A working model was constructed by James D. Watson and Francis H. C. Crick. Each received the Nobel Prize. See James D. Watson: *The Double Helix: A Personal Account of the Discovery of the Structure of DNA.* New York, Atheneum, 1968.

anticipated in the evolutionary literature). His religious motives for forming these particular concepts, rather than other alternatives represented by other philosophers of evolution, are obvious to any critical reader. It is not his scientific descriptions that are called into question, but his *interpretation* of established facts. To be sure, his philosophy of evolution represents a bold attempt to reconcile science and faith. But it must be demonstrated that faith is, in fact, *necessary* to correctly interpret planetary evolution without misinterpreting the established facts and therefore misinterpreting the process. It is clear that Teilhard has given preference to faith over science. Ultimately, he relied upon knowledge by Connaturality. Typical of religious thinkers, he uses faith to understand.

As a theologian, Teilhard believed in a personal God, the immortality of the human soul, freedom of the human will, and gave a cosmic interpretation of Christ and Original Sin. For the most part, his theology is a Christology (the universe, i.e. cosmogenesis, is Christocentric). His demythologization and secularization of the Church reached their limit at the relevance of Christ.[73] He presented the historical figure of Jesus of Nazareth as Christ the Cosmic Pantokrator. The Incarnation, Redemption, and Consummation took on a cosmic and evolutionary perspective. In short, evolution is fulfilled and totalized only in and through a cosmic Christ. Christ *is* Evolution, the immanent nature of God-Omega within a converging panentheism.

The evolution of the universe finds its stability ahead and above in a divine Personal Center. God-Omega gives unity, movement, direction, and purpose to cosmogenesis by being the absolute and divine focus and end of a personalizing, teleological, and converging process. But Teilhard taught that Christ himself

---

[73]For a study of the religious thought of Pierre Teilhard de Chardin, see Henri de Lubac: *The Religion of Teilhard de Chardin.* New York, Desclee Company, 1967; Christopher F. Mooney: *Teilhard de Chardin and the Mystery of Christ.* New York, Harper and Row, 1966; and Emile Rideau: *Teilhard de Chardin: A Guide to His Thought.* London, Collins, 1967.

is both the immanent and transcendent center of the Universe. For God-Omega and Christ become one at the completion of time.

It is clear that Teilhard's Christian faith has greatly influenced his historico-phenomenological analysis of planetary evolution and colored his interpretation. Scientific facts have been supplemented by faith. But theological presuppositions must never be allowed to predetermine what is to be admissible as scientific evidence concerning natural phenomena. Faith is always subject to the established knowledge of the special sciences. As such, one's personal views grounded in faith cannot be submitted as the true interpretation of the whole universe. The advances of the sciences have repeatedly forced religious thinkers to modify their positions. And we may safely assume that this will continue to be true in the future. How could there be a final system or *philosophia perennis* in an evolving universe which we may safely assume to be eternal, infinitely infinite, and open to unlimited possibilities? It is dogmatic to place closure on the universe or human inquiry.

As a mystic, Teilhard held that his experiences, whether scientific, philosophical, or theological, substantiated the ultimate spiritual unity of reality (a concept which permeates all of his thought). In general, he taught the unity of the geosphere, biosphere, and noosphere. And geogenesis, biogenesis, and noogenesis represented single but successive planetary movements of one unitary process. In particular, he taught the unity of cosmic evolution and the autonomy of a Personal Center. Drawing his mystical experiences to their ultimate conclusion, he prophesied the eventual union of evolution or Christ with God-Omega at the Omega-Point, i.e. converging panentheism would eventually resolve itself in a true pantheism. In short, Teilhard's personal vision is fundamentally a mystical vision which cannot be symbolized, communicated, or verified.

B. TEILHARD AND FEUERBACH

It is surprising that while Teilhard advocated an evolutionary perspective, he never seriously considered the historical development of religions. There are psychological, anthropological, and sociological arguments for the origin of religious beliefs.

In *The Essence of Christianity* (1841), Ludwig Feuerbach (1804-1872) adopted a materialistic position. He saw theology as mystical, perverted Anthropology, imaginary psychology, and esoteric pathology. It was responsible for the dichotomy between God who is infinite, perfect, eternal, omnipotent, and holy and man who is finite, imperfect, temporal, weak, and sinful. In short, he held that Theology should be replaced by a true Anthropology.

Feuerbach taught that theological beliefs in a personal God, personal immortality of the human soul, freedom of the human will, Heaven, the Incarnation and Resurrection, miracles, prayer, and revelation are merely the realizations of human wishes of the heart. The essence of faith is the idea that that which man wishes actually is. He taught that theological ideas are the products of man's subjective nature, and as a result religion is grounded in human feelings and emotions rather than metaphysical correlates. In short, Theology is the objectification of the imagination of the heart and not a product of understanding.

In *Principles of the Philosophy of the Future* (1843), Feuerbach advocated a *new philosophy*, a philosophical anthropology which was fundamentally antitheological. He claimed that the idea of a personal God was a deceit perpetuated by the privileged class. Likewise, theology is anthropomorphic for God's attributes are merely the projection of human attributes or qualities. In short, man was the beginning, middle, and end of religion.

In *Lectures on the Essence of Religion* (1848), Feuerbach summarized his life's investigation into the origin of Theology:

> Only in direct communion with nature can man become whole again, can he cast aside all extravagant, supernatural, and unnatural ideas and fantasies. . . . In theology things are not thought and willed because they exist, they exist because they are thought and willed. . . . God and religion are nothing more than man's yearning for happiness, satisfied in his imagination.[74]

---

[74]Ludwig Feuerbach: *Lectures on the Essence of Religion.* New York, Harper and Row, 1967, pp. 4, 117, 246.

Neither Feuerbach nor Teilhard have given a rigorous philosophical anthropology or critical study of man's place in nature.
Feuerbach's interpretation gave a passive view of human individuals and retained a relational concept of God (God is the
result of the interrelationships between a collective mankind). It
lacked an objective, practico-critical concern for historical and
social activity or *praxis*. And it failed to emphasize that the "religious feeling" of individuals is itself a historico-social product.
Nevertheless, Feuerbach does represent a chronological and philosophical link between Hegel and Marx. (Marx rightly rejected
Feuerbach's relational concept of God and passive interpretation
of man.)

Teilhard's position is even less satisfactory, for it is grounded
in theism. A rigorous phenomenology of evolution which em-
braces the development of culture will clearly disclose that human
individuals themselves have constituted the concept of a transcendent world of Being with its objects as a result of human needs,
values, and desires. Likewise, human individuals have constituted
systems of theology, philosophy, mathematics, and logic.

Those blindly enthusiastic over Teilhard's thought would do
well to seriously consider Feuerbach's position.

C. TEILHARD AND WHITEHEAD

There are great similarities and differences between the
thoughts of Teilhard and Alfred North Whitehead (1861-1947).
In their own fashion, both cosmologies have contributed to
science-oriented process philosophy. Unlike Teilhard's synthesis
which originated from evolutionary biology supported by his field
work in geology and paleontology, Whitehead's metaphysics resulted from a rigorous concern for the influences of relativity
physics, quantum theory, the philosophy of science, mathematics,
and logic on a modern understanding and conceptualization of
nature. (One recalls the different orientations of Aristotle and
Plato respectively.) The doctrine of evolution remained implicit
rather than explicit in Whitehead's speculations.

Whitehead's *Science and the Modern World* (1925) is a series of lectures devoted to the development of Western science and philosophy during the last three centuries (a consideration of epistemology is admittedly entirely excluded). From Copernicus and Bruno to modern ideas in physics and biology, he showed that the growth of science directly influences conceptual frameworks. But because of the Cartesian philosophy of dualism, scientific inquiry had concentrated upon subjective analysis. (The latter position is especially illustrated in the works of Leibniz, Kant, Hegel, and Husserl.) But for Whitehead, a process cosmology must do justice to objective and subjective realms of inquiry. In short, a modern cosmology must do justice to scientific, philosophical, and religious or aesthetic experience without a bifurcation of nature.

Whitehead's Philosophy of Organism is a philosophy of nature dealing with the essentials, and called for a reinterpretation of the following notions: God, Space, Time, Mind, Matter, Change, Endurance, Causality, Eternality, Interfusion, Organism, Order, and Value. And Whitehead presented the "Fallacy of Misplaced Concreteness," i.e. "the accidental error of mistaking the abstract for the concrete."[75] (The author holds that Whitehead himself had committed this fallacy, and contributed confusion to his future system.)

In *Religion in the Making* (1926), Whitehead presented a very general introduction to his future synthesis. Looking at the historical development of religions, he pointed out that the pantheism of Buddhism and the theism of Christianity resulted from an immanent and transcendental treatment of God respectively. Like Teilhard, he desired to synthesize science, philosophy, and theology within a rational panentheism (for Whitehead, rational religion originates in the solitariness of the individual in community, and is grounded in a penetrating sincerity):

> You cannot shelter theology from science, or science from theology; nor can you shelter either of them from metaphysics, or metaphysics from either of them. There is no short cut to truth. . . . Science

---

[75]Alfred North Whitehead: *Science and the Modern World*. New York, Macmillan, 1967, p. 51.

suggested a cosmology; and whatever suggests a cosmology, suggests a religion.[76]

Whitehead's major work is *Process and Reality: An Essay in Cosmology* (1929). It is a systematic presentation of his Philosophy of Organism, and a work which is considerably more difficult to follow than Teilhard's *The Phenomenon of Man*. It is a tentative, descriptive generalization of Nature as a totality, emphasizing the aesthetic feelings generated as the result of the adventure of creative experience. The system is rational, empirical, and employs the free imagination controlled by the requirements of coherence and logic.

Whitehead repeatedly emphasized that speculative philosophy should be coherent, logical, applicative, and adequate to deal with the facts of immediate actual experience. Science-oriented, Whitehead's work attempted to handle the creativity, novelty, and interrelatedness of the present cosmic epoch. The universe is represented as fields of interrelated atomic events manifesting degrees of mental activity (feelings) within an ordered creative advance toward novelty and subjective satisfaction. The creative advance of Nature is Life or fields of activity manifesting teleological aims toward the future enjoyment of emotions.

Again reminding us of Plato, Whitehead's system incorporates into unity three formative elements: (a) Creativity as the endless advance of actual occasions, entities, or events toward novelty; (b) Ideal Forms, Eternal Objects, or Potentials; (c) God. The self-realizing actual occasions are structured societies or nexūs of feelings or prehensions within a continuous flux.

The Philosophy of Organism was an attempt to describe the creative plurality and essential unity of the world. Whitehead wrote:

In the actual world we discern four grades of actual occasions, grades which are not to be sharply distinguished from each other. First, and lowest, there are the actual occasions in so-called "empty space;"

secondly, there are the actual occasions which are moments in the life-histories of enduring non-living objects, such as electrons or other primitive organisms; thirdly, there are the actual occasions which are moments in the life-histories of enduring living objects; fourthly, there are the actual occasions which are moments in the life-histories of enduring objects with conscious knowledge. . . . The oneness of the universe, and the oneness of each element in the universe, repeat themselves to the crack of doom in the creative advance from creature to creature, each creature including in itself the whole of history and exemplifying the self-identity of things and their mutual diversities.[77]

He rejected a bifurcation of Nature, but held to the dipolarity of each actual entity in the process of becoming, i.e. each entity has a mental and physical pole.

God is held to be the chief exemplification of all metaphysical principles. He is eternal, immanent, self-consistent, and transcends any finite cosmic epoch. As an actual entity, God is also dipolar (Whitehead wrote of the Primordial and Consequent natures of God). The Primordial nature or conceptual experience of God is the "Object of desire" of the eternal urge of the universe (recall Aristotle's Unmoved Mover and Plato's Goodness). This aspect of God is His unlimited potentiality, i.e. it is the realm of the Eternal Objects. While the Consequent nature or physical experience of God is the finite, fluent multiplicity of the World.

God and the World are ontologically interrelated through a reciprocal relationship of everlasting Creativity seeking a perfected unity. The existence, stability, order, creative advance, novelty, purpose, and value of the World are dependent upon Him. (There is clearly an attempt to save a personal conception of God.) But Whitehead has not been intellectually honest. The author believes that a materialistic pantheism is the only acceptable position capable of doing rational justice to an aesthetic appreciation of the infinite unity of the physical universe.

Where Teilhard moved from matter to energy to spirit,

---

[77]Alfred North Whitehead: *Process and Reality: An Essay in Cosmology.* New York, Macmillan, 1969, pp. 205, 266.

Whitehead moved from matter to energy to aesthetic experience. (There is a need for a *practical* and *functional* account of human experience in all of its modes, remembering that such experience is a recent, natural event.) Both philosophers reacted against dogmatic mechanistic materialism by presenting science-oriented, organismic views of process and progress. Their cosmologies emphasized creativity, novelty, and the increasing complexity and consciousness manifested in Nature. And both systems were panpsychic, vitalistic, teleological, and panentheistic.

The author sympathizes with Teilhard's and Whitehead's struggle to construct a new terminology to convey new ideas and meanings which have not been previously found in traditional philosophy. New cosmic, evolutionary, and mentalistic vocabularies are needed in light of new perspectives and established facts.

But there are major differences between these two cosmologies. Where Teilhard taught a monistic, converging, finalistic Universe grounded in traditional theism, Whitehead presented a pluralistic, diverging, eternal Nature grounded in a form of panentheism.

A philosophical system may be coherent and profound while not sound. It must be remembered that the cosmologist and his system are historically and socially conditioned. Whitehead's tentative cosmology, with its reliance upon intuitions and assumptive reasoning, is far removed from the data of actual human experience and the corpus of established facts. Its speculations are idealistic for ontologically a privileged position has been given to experience in general, and feelings in particular.

Knowledge from all of the special sciences is necessary for a proper interpretation of the place of human experience within an infinite universe. A broad form of naturalism can interpret the physical world and human experience without appealing to idealistic constructions which are inevitably religious in motivation. There is no need to resort to supernatural or transcendent causes. Scientific and philosophical inquiry imply a cosmology, but a cosmology does not necessitate religious assumptions. It has yet to be demonstrated that God is a *necessary* and *indispensable* entity for any sound philosophical system that attempts to do justice to reality.

The value of rigorous metaphysical inquiry is obvious to scientists and philosophers. But the abstract and aesthetic approach of Whitehead's cosmology may be irrelevant to the critical problems now prevalent in the human condition. The author maintains that a cosmic and historically oriented materialism which remains open to the further advances of the special sciences is capable of doing justice to reality, experience, and human values.

D. TEILHARD AND HUMANISM

Hegel held that the dialectical, progressive unfolding of social history toward greater freedom, unity, and reason represented the Absolute Spirit or God eternally actualizing its potentialities. He had adopted a position of objective idealism. As a result the objective problems of man were ignored by an excessive concern for the Absolute, which was held to be more than a concept because of his use of the principle of identity (the distinction between epistemology and ontology is crucial if a correct understanding of experience and reality is desired). Feuerbach and Marx rightly reacted against this idealism and lack of humanism, i.e. Hegel's disregard for the concrete world and actual men. Their insights cannot be ignored.

Teilhard was a humanist concerned for the future welfare of the human phylum. He gives us a *Christian* humanism in which man and God work together to prepare the earth for the Parousia and Pleroma. It is his faith in the potentialities of a collective mankind that we can admire. He taught that a decrease in egoism resulted in an increase of altruism (persons find themselves, i.e. give meaning to their lives, by losing themselves in their work). Certainly we need a philosophy of work.

A humanistic naturalism can retain Teilhard's concern for a collective *praxis* without the theological support. His optimism and faith in the future is sorely needed today. And his position has been an inspiration to many. His concern for human survival is more urgent today than it was when he wrote his synthesis.

Teilhard desired to establish a science of human energetics, a true anthropology which he referred to as an Ultra-Physics or Ultra-Anthropology. Such a science would synthesize the knowledge of the natural, social, formal, and conceptual sciences in order to direct the future development of the human phylum. A naturalist may whole-heartedly embrace this hope. The author believes we may safely assume that the twenty-first century will be an Age of Synthesis.

There are existential and Marxist elements in Teilhard's thought. He was aware of the excessive anguish and detachments within the world. He had seen two cosmic directions: (a) converging evolution and (b) entropy. Likewise, he saw two possible options for the future direction of hominization: (a) success or (b) failure. Ultimately, Teilhard argued that on the theological level of interpretation the success of the human phylum was guaranteed by God-Omega. Yet his thought has opened the road for a Marxist-Christian dialogue, i.e. there is the possibility of a genuine intellectual cooperation between Marxists and Christians. Yet it is obvious that the two philosophies are fundamentally contradictory.[78]

For Teilhard, Christianity is a religion of action and not merely a passive faith resisting the inevitable movement of nature toward the unification and liberation of psychic energy. One may safely say that Teilhardism is the most significant direction of thought currently in Catholicism. But where it teaches that scientific activity is ultimately spiritual activity, the Marxists hold

---

[78]For a consideration of Teilhardism by a Marxist, see Roger Garaudy: *From Anathema to Dialogue: A Marxist Challenge to the Christian Churches.* New York, Random House, 1968.

that science is bringing about the rejection of religion, superstition, magic, and myth.

The author believes that Teilhard's own attempt at a synthesis of science and faith shows clearly that theology cannot be supported by the special sciences alone. In the last analysis, there is a profound divergence between Marxism and Christianity which Teilhardism is incapable of bridging.

E. FINAL INTERPRETATION

Teilhard has not given us a *rigorous* phenomenology of planetary evolution, for he has not limited himself to a critical description of natural and social phenomena. His historico-phenomenology of evolution is a description of the essential structures and relationships within the process as well as a consideration of purpose and inner meaning. But his synthesis of all of the aspects of reality is Christian, and as such what we have is essentially a Christian metaphysics of dialectical spiritualism conditioned by eschatological considerations and grounded in mysticism.

Teilhard's phenomenology of evolution is neither scientifically defensible nor a necessary consequence of a philosophical description and analysis of nature. It must be noted that a naturalistic phenomenology is capable of doing justice to all that is scientifically verifiable in his thought.

The evolution of Teilhard's own thought was consistent, for at no time in his life did he make any significant change in his Christian interpretation of evolution. His life was clearly devoted to clarifying and scientifically verifying, whenever possible, the cosmic vision he had first intuited while completing his theological and scientific studies.

To properly evaluate Teilhard's thought we must draw up a balance sheet, i.e. we must consider his shortcomings as well as his contributions to an understanding of man's place in the universe. There is much which is confusing, ambiguous, and erroneous in his synthesis. (We have already seen that his spiritual monism, vitalism, Law of increasing centro-Complexity-Consciousness, and critical thresholds have been anticipated in the evolutionary literature. And they are unwarranted conceptions to support a theological position.) It is unfortunate that he did not develop a rigorous methodology, evolutionary logic, and ethics. To be sure, no single human being can do justice to all realms of inquiry.

Teilhard did not limit himself to the self-correcting method of the special sciences, or to the accumulative, established knowledge of the sciences. His synthesis of distinct levels of interpretation supplements the empirical, hypothetico-deductive method of the sciences with philosophical, theological, and mystical assumptions. It is true that the process of evolution in the past has to be inferred, yet all the scientific evidence points to the fact that the same evolutionary principles operating today have guided evolution in the past. It is in the explanation and interpretation of evolution that differences of opinion have arisen.

One may challenge a particular interpretation, but to contest the interpretation is not to deny the validity of the process itself. It is a fallacy to discredit the truth of evolution by pointing out the disagreements concerning the mechanism of evolution and its meaning. Where modern Darwinism emphasizes accidental variations, environmental circumstances, and sees evolution as an indefinite sequence of indifferent results, Teilhardism tries to justify transcendent causality, rational order within process, purpose, and direction. But there is no empirical evidence to support Teilhardism. It relies upon religious and mystical intuitions to supplement empirical evidence in order to construct a dialectical system between the real and the conceptual. The danger of such a philosophy is that it may misrepresent the facticity and complexity of concrete reality.

To do justice to Teilhard's thought, we must also recognize its merits. He has given us a perspective that is seldom presented in current philosophical literature. Although he did not develop a rigorous methodology or labor over linguistic problems, he did obtain a cosmic perspective to the degree that he acknowledged that man and the earth are only a small aspect of the indeterminate expansion of the universe. Such a perspective prevented him from establishing a myopic vision so present in contemporary thought which is seemingly analytic for the sake of analysis with little or no concern for implications or practicality. From the Greeks to the present, naturalistic or science-oriented philosophies have emphasized the need to relate conceptual frameworks to physical existence (no closure should be placed upon rigorous mathematical and logical inquiries that may prove applicable in the future).

Teilhard was concerned with content and action. Despite his personal persecutions, he never turned from the human milieu and his research. As his thought matured, the present problems of the human condition became his major concern. And the cosmic perspective which he developed was a source of seemingly endless inspiration. If Teilhard loved the cosmos, he loved the earth with its evolutionary potentialities even more. His cosmic orientation was merely a modern acknowledgment of the expansion of human knowledge. Unlike Bruno, he did not dwell upon the infinity of the cosmos, but narrowed and focused his considerations to the earth.

Not only had many philosophers and theologians neglected to consider the infinite universe, but they also rejected an evolutionary framework. In general, what makes Teilhard's philosophy modern is its acceptance of evolution as a basic fact. It was one thing for scientists to work within an evolutionary model, and quite another for a Jesuit-priest to explicitly advocate the fact of evolution as an *a priori* condition of all natural and social phenomena including the Christ. Yet it is to Teilhard's credit that once he saw the validity of evolution he did not recant his personal views under the pressures of his Church (recall the unfortunate treatment of Galileo).

Many contemporary process philosophers speak of creative development within metaphysical abstractions without appealing to the natural and social facts to substantiate their positions. Teilhard's broad and deep grasp of scientific knowledge kept his feet, for the most part, firmly planted on the ground. It is unfortunate that his concern for eschatology prevented him from developing a truly cosmic vision. In short, we do not have a modern cosmology, yet the seeds for such a perspective are in his vision. One result of his life's work is that many, inspired by his thoughts, will extend his vision to a naturalistic, cosmic dimension.

Teilhard was a man of flesh and blood. From his letters we learn of his love for travel, passion for revealing man's past, and see him reading Sartre and Toynbee, listening to Beethoven and Wagner, relishing autumn days, and always maintaining a deep concern for the future destiny of man. We also learn of his limits in understanding mathematics as well as his poor acquaintance with recorded history. His extensive traveling had brought him in contact with peoples from literally all over the globe. Yet his optimism and bold vision were never shakened or diminished.

Nietzsche had written:

> The dangers for a philosopher's development are indeed so manifold today that one may doubt whether this fruit can still ripen at all. The scope and the tower-building of the sciences has grown to be enormous, and with this also the probability that the philosopher grows weary while still learning or allows himself to be detained somewhere to become a "specialist"—so he never attains his proper level, the height for a comprehensive look, for looking around, for looking *down*.[79]

The author believes that Teilhard had reached such a desired height, and wrote a work that is descriptive, interpretive, and prescriptive. And since no single human being can master all of the knowledge of his time, it is remarkable that he achieved such a degree of comprehension. One wonders what his views would

---

[79]Friedrich Nietzsche: *Beyond Good and Evil*. New York, Random House, 1966, p. 124.

have been had he had greater freedom in which to develop and express himself.

Concerning his bold attempt at a synthesis, Teilhard wrote:

In this arrangement of values I may have gone astray at many points. It is up to others to try to do better. My one hope is that I have made the reader feel both the reality, difficulty, and urgency of the problem and, at the same time, the scale and the form which the solution cannot escape. . . . In one manner or other it still remains true that, even in the view of the mere biologist, the human epic resembles nothing so much as a way of the Cross.[80]

How may we summarize the significance of the Teilhardian synthesis? (We have already seen that his philosophy of evolution is, in part, scientifically unwarranted and philosophically unconvincing. This is due to his theological and planetary orientation.) His contributions as a scientist cannot compare to those of Galileo, Newton, Darwin, or Einstein. And as a philosopher, he cannot rank with Leibniz, Kant, Hegel, or Husserl. In short, he belongs with those all too few philosophers who have taken the doctrine of evolution and its implications seriously.

Teilhard's fundamental concepts are not empirical discoveries but merely personal ideas which the author maintains will not be accepted as having lasting value for the established body of reliable scientific knowledge. He has given a theologically oriented conceptual framework or interpretation of planetary evolution and not an explanation subject to verification. In fact, the author also maintains that further scientific inquiry will result in the abandonment of the Teilhardian synthesis in favor of a rigorous naturalistic interpretation of man's origin and development in the cosmos.

In the final analysis, Teilhard's synthesis has not resolved the real dichotomies between religion and science. Yet his serious recognition of evolution will remain a landmark in the history of evolutionary thought. His sincere and bold attempt to reconcile evolution and theism will rather tend to increase the acceptance

---

[80]*The Phenomenon of Man*, pp. 290, 313.

of the scientific conception of evolution over orthodox Christianity and mysticism. Hopefully, the natural descent or ascent of man from Miocene hominoids will be recognized as scientifically true.

TEILHARD'S WORKS IN ENGLISH[81]

TEILHARD DE CHARDIN, PIERRE

1956 The antiquity and world expansion of human culture. *Man's Role in Changing the Face of the Earth.* pp. 103-112. Edited by William L. Thomas, Jr. The University of Chicago Press, Chicago.

1962 The idea of fossil man. *Anthropology Today: Selections*, pp. 31-38. Edited by Sol Tax. The University of Chicago Press, Chicago.

1965 *Building the Earth.* Translated by Noël Lindsay. Dimension Books, Inc., Wilkes-Barre, Pennsylvania.

Hymn of the Universe. Translated by Simon Bartholomew. Harper and Row, Publishers, New York.

Letters From Egypt: 1905-1908. Translated by Mary Ilford. Herder and Herder, New York.

The Appearance of Man. Translated by J. M. Cohen. Harper and Row, Publishers, New York.

The Making of a Mind: Letters From a Soldier-Priest 1914-1919. Translated by René Hague. Harper and Row, Publishers, New York.

The Phenomenon of Man. 2nd ed. Translated by Bernard Wall. Harper and Row, Publishers, New York.

1966 *Man's Place in Nature: The Human Zoological Group.* Translated by René Hague. Harper and Row, Publishers, New York.

The Vision of the Past. Translated by J. M. Cohen. Harper and Row, Publishers, New York.

1967 *Letters From Paris: 1912-1914.* Translated by Michael Mazzarese. Herder and Herder, New York.

1968 *Letters From a Traveller.* Translated by Bernard Wall. Harper and Row, Publishers, New York.

Letters From Hastings: 1908-1912. Translated by Judith de Stefano. Herder and Herder, New York.

Letters to Two Friends: 1926-1952. Translated by Helen Weaver. The New American Library, Inc., New York.

Science and Christ. Translated by René Hague. Harper and Row, Publishers, New York.

The Divine Milieu. Rev. ed. Translated by Bernard Wall. Harper and Row, Publishers, New York.

---

[81]For a recent, comprehensive bibliography on evolution, see H. J. Birx and E. B. Ehrle: Organic evolution: Selections from the literature. *BioScience: 20* (8, 10, 12, 14, 16, 18, 20, 24), *21* (2, 4).

Writings in Time of War. Translated by René Hague. Harper and Row, Publishers, New York.

1969 *How I Believe.* Translated by René Hague. Harper and Row, Publishers, New York.

Letters to Leontine Zanta. Translated by Bernard Wall. Harper and Row, Publishers, New York.

The Future of Man. Translated by Norman Denny. Harper and Row, Publishers, New York.

1970 *Activation of Energy.* Translated by René Hague. Harcourt Brace Jovanovich, New York.

Human Energy. Translated by J. M. Cohen. Harcourt Brace Jovanovich, New York.

1971 *Christianity and Evolution.* Translated by René Hague. Harcourt Brace Jovanovich, New York.

INDEX

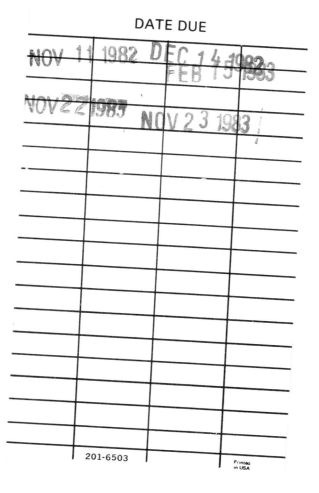